THE
AMERICAN
COVENANT

THE UNTOLD STORY

BY
MARSHALL FOSTER
AND
MARY-ELAINE SWANSON

For information on purchasing additional copies of this book, ordering copies of the Study Leader's Guide designed for use with it, or subscribing to the bi-monthly Mayflower Institute Journal, write to the Foundation for Christian Self-Government, P. O. Box 1087, Thousand Oaks, Ca. 91360.

Color photography by Plimoth Plantation, Plymouth, MA

Table of Contents

THE SIGNING OF THE MAYFLOWER COMPACT (1620)
BY PERCY MORAN

MAYFLOWER COMPACT 1620

In y name of god Amen· we whose names are underwriten
the loyall subiects of our dread soueraigne Lord King Iames
by y grace of god, of great Britaine, franc, & yreland king.
defendor of y faith, &c

Haueing undertaken, for y glorie of god, and aduancements
of y christian, and honour of our king & countrie, a voyage to
plant y first colonie in y Northerne parts of virginia· doe
by these presents solemnly & mutualy in y presence of god, and
one of another, Couenant, & Combine our selues togeather into a
Ciuill body politick; for our better ordering, & preseruation & furtherance of y ends aforesaid; and by vertue hearof to enacte,
constitute, and frame such iust & equall Lawes, ordinances,
Acts, constitutions, & offices, from time to time, as shall be thought
most meete & conuenient for y generall good of y Colonie: unto
which we promise all due submission and obedience. yn witnes
wherof we haue here under subscribed our names at Cap=
Codd y ·11· of Nouember in y year of y raigne of our soueraigne
Lord king Iames of England, franc, & yreland y eighteenth
and of scotland y fiftie fourth Anᵒ: Dom. 1620·]

IN the Name of God, Amen. We whose Names
are under-written, the Loyal Subjects of our dread
Soveraign Lord King James, by the grace of God of
Great Brettain, France and Ireland, King, Defender of the
Faith, &c. Having undertaken for the glory of God,
and advancement of the Christian Faith, and the Honour of our King and Countrey, a Voyage to plant the
first Colony in the Northern parts of Virginia; Do by
these Presents solemnly and mutually, in the presence of
God and one another, Covenant and Combine our
selves together into a Civil Body Politick, for our better
ordering and preservation, and furtherance of the ends
aforesaid; and by virtue hereof do enact, constitute and
frame such just and equal Laws, Ordinances, Acts, Constitutions and Officers, from time to time, as shall be
thought most meet and convenient for the general good
of the Colony; unto which we promise all due submission and obedience. In witness whereof we have here-
unto subscribed our Names at Cape Cod, the eleventh of
November, in the Reign of our Soveraign Lord King
James, of England, France and Ireland the eighteenth,
and of Scotland the fifty fourth, Anno Dom. 1620.

This was the first Foundation of the Govern-ment of New-Plimouth.

John Carver.	Samuel Fuller.	Edward Tilly.
William Bradford.	Christopher Martin.	John Tilly.
Edward Winslow.	William Mullins.	Francis Cook.
William Brewster.	William White.	Thomas Rogers.
Isaac Allerton.	Richard Warren.	Thomas Tinker.
Miles Standish.	John Howland.	John Ridgdale.
John Alden.	Steven Hopkins.	Edward Fuller.
John Turner.	Digery Priest.	Richard Clark.
Francis Eaton.	Thomas Williams.	Richard Gardiner.
James Chilton.	Gilbert Winslow.	John Allerton.
John Craxton.	Edmund Margeson.	Thomas English.
John Billington.	Peter Brown.	Edward Doten.
Joses Fletcher.	Richard Bitteridge.	Edward Liester.
John Goodman.	George Soule.	

GOVERNOR BRADFORD'S COPY OF THE MAYFLOWER COMPACT
Preserved in his handwriting in his History of Plymouth Plantation,

OVER 300 YEARS AGO!

The "Compact", with the signers, as first
printed in "Morton's Memorial" at Cambridge,
Mass., in 1669, an official publication of the
Plymouth Colony. The order of signing the original manuscript is not known.

Foreword

What is The American Covenant?

Few people in history have been as self-flagellating as the American emerging from the decade of the seventies. The people who astounded the world for two centuries with their hope and enthusiasm suddenly seemed rudderless, losing themselves in soap operas and superbowls, but sensing deep within an impending collapse. Even those in power, who often had preached a Pollyanna message of future glory, declared that we as a people were experiencing a "national malaise."

It seemed as though the loose-knit coalition of secular values was coming apart in the "me generation." Time-Life publications examined this phenomenon in detail in a special project called The American Renewal. In the March 1982 edition of *Life*, Henry Grunwald summarizes well our dilemma.

> *"The belief in an ever-better tomorrow, the conviction that obstacles exist to overcome and that the U.S. has a strong and beneficial role to play in the world — these constitute the American secular religion. For some time now, that religion has been corroded by doubt. Intractable inflation seems to have turned the good life into a treadmill and shaken our confidence in the future — America's last frontier. Our industry appears to have lost its productive magic, its daring, and sometimes even its competence. Our government is intrusive, inept — and expensive. Our democracy too often produces mediocrity and deadlock."*[1]

The Dying Secular Religious Consensus

To understand our present condition we need to come to grips with the fact that we have fallen away from the original American Covenant of our Founding Fathers for the last 150 years. Most of us are so far away from it that we didn't even know it existed and formed the foundation of our nation.

Layer upon layer of secularized translations of this covenant have obscured the true meaning and culturally regenerating nature of the covenants and compacts of our early settlers. As often happens when generations pass and prosperity comes, the deeply religious foundation for our national blessings has been forgotten. In the early nineteenth century, the Christian community, which had been the dominant cultural force for two hundred years, began to ignore its responsibilities. Compromising voices came forth to explain the greatness of America as a "manifest destiny." We were born to rule, some postulated. Others said we were a "chosen race." The voices of Christians who were needed to expose such blatant error were muffled by a growing ignorance of our heritage.

In this century politicians and others have tried to rally the American patriot under the banner of democracy, the Great Society, or the American Renewal. But all these attempts have failed or will fail to change our national direction and unite our people, for they are built upon the shifting sands of secular humanism and lead only to apathy and ultimately to defeat.

We as a people have forgotten that our foundations were laid upon the Rock of Ages. Daniel Webster acknowledged this truth. Speaking at Plymouth, Massachusetts on December 22, 1820, at the bicentennial of the founding of Plymouth, he ended his address with this admonition:

"Finally, let us not forget the religious character of our origin. Our fathers were brought hither by their high veneration for the Christian religion. They journeyed by its light, and labored in its hope. They sought to incorporate its principles with the elements of their society, and to diffuse its influence through all their institutions, civil, political, or literary. Let us cherish these sentiments, and extend this influence still more widely; in the full conviction, that that is the happiest society which partakes in the highest degree of the mild and peaceful spirit of Christianity." (CHOC, p. 248)

Defining Covenant

The word covenant is not in common usage today as it was at the time of our founding. A covenant, in those days, was a solemn agreement, signed or not, between individuals or between God and an individual, a church or a nation.

Our founders understood the power of covenants because they were Biblicists. They knew that God would inevitably act in accordance with His Word if the human covenanter would obey His Word. They also knew that this truth of blessing was applicable to a nation as well as to an individual. Deuteronomy 7:9 says: *"Know therefore that the Lord thy God, He is God, the faithful God, which keepeth covenant and mercy with them that love Him and keep His commandments to a thousand generations."*

The American Covenant

The study you have embarked upon will give you first-hand knowledge of the covenant of our forefathers which reveals the fundamental reason America has been blessed. The self-governing Christians known as Pilgrims who wrote the Mayflower Compact were aboard the Mayflower at the time of its writing surveying a desolate wilderness in the dead of winter. Persecuted in England for their religious convictions, they had spent 12 difficult years of exile in Holland and now had arrived on the wild New England Coast to begin a colony for the "glorie of God." But even as the Mayflower rode at anchor, they knew that before setting foot in the New World, they had to draw up this covenant before God because they feared launching their colony until there was a recognition of God's sovereignty and the need to obey Him. The Mayflower Compact is America's first great constitutional document.

The Mayflower Compact

"In ye name of God, Amen. We whose names are underwriten, the loyall subjects of our dread soveraigne Lord, King James, by ye grace of God, of Great Britaine, France, & Ireland king, defender of ye faith, &c., haveing undertaken, for ye glorie of God, and advancemente of ye Christian faith, and honour of our king & countrie, a voyage to plant ye first colonie in ye Northerne parts of Virginia, doe by these presents solemnly & mutually in ye presence of God, and one of another, covenant & combine our selves togeather into a civill body politick, for our better ordering & preservation & furtherance of ye ends aforesaid; and by vertue hearof to enacte, constitute, and frame such just & equall lawes, ordinances, acts, constitutions & offices, from time to time, as shall be thought most meete & convenient for ye generall good of ye Colonie, unto which we promise all due submission and obedience. In witnes wherof we have hereunder subscribed our names at Cap-Codd ye 11. of November, in ye year of ye raigne of our soveraigne lord, King James, of England, France, & Ireland ye eighteenth, and by Scotland ye fiftie fourth. Ano:Dom. 1620." (CHOC, p. 204-205)

These serious vows were echoed by colony after colony, church after church, as we moved toward nationhood.

According to Professor Andrew McLaughlin's *"Foundations of American Constitutionalism,"* *"...the word 'covenant' and its significance will appear over and over again as we trace the development of American constitutional theory..."*[2]

Our Declaration of Independence ends with the acknowledgment of the sovereignty of God in which the Founders, in effect, covenanted together to form a nation: *"And for the support of this Declaration, with a firm reliance on the Protection of divine Providence, we mutually pledge to each other our Lives, our Fortunes, and our sacred Honor."*

Political scientist Daniel J. Elazar, Director of the Center for the Study of Federalism, Temple University, Philadelphia, and associated with Bar Ilan University, Israel, writes that "just as the heart of the covenant of ancient Israel consists of two parts, the Decalogue or Ten Commandments with its electrifying statement of fundamental principles and the Book of the Covenant with its more detailed framework of basic laws of the Israelite Commonwealth, so too does that of the American covenant consist of two basic documents serving the same purposes – the Declaration of Independence and the Constitution."[3]

Reaffirming our Covenant

If there is to be a real American renewal, it will have to begin through a repentant reaffirmation of our American Covenant. God blessed our fathers because they covenanted, agreed, contracted with God to obey His Son (Psalm 2:10). God has not changed His purpose for America but we, as Americans, have forgotten our covenant, our response to His purpose.

The Hope of America

The real hope of America is in the return of God's people to their corporate as well as individual covenant with their God. The following chapters will detail the untold story of how this covenant came about and how it can be renewed so that America can be used as a vessel of honor by God, rather than as a vessel of wrath, for the spreading of His Gospel to the world.

"Be wise now therefore, O ye kings: be instructed, ye judges of the earth. Serve the Lord with fear, and rejoice with trembling. Kiss the son, lest He be angry, and ye perish from the way, when His wrath is kindled but a little. Blessed are all they that put their trust in Him." (Psalm 2:10-12)

Notes:

1. "American Renewal" by Henry Grunwald, LIFE ©1981 Time Inc. All rights reserved.
2. Andrew D. McLaughlin, *The Foundations of American Constitutionalism* (New York University, 1932; New York: Fawcett World Library, 1961), p.19.
3. Daniel J. Elazar, "From Biblical Covenant To Modern Federalism: The Federal Theology Bridge," *Workshop on Covenant and Politics* (Philadelphia: Center for the Study of Federalism, Temple University, 1980), p. 17.

Preface

*T*he American Covenant – *The Untold Story*, has been designed as an
introduction to America's Christian history showing its relevance to this
nation's future. It is based on more than 25 years of research in the field of
American history and is keyed to two invaluable volumes produced by Verna
M. Hall and Rosalie J. Slater. We are indebted to them for their pioneer work
in uncovering the rich vein of long-hidden documentation on our American
Christian heritage. Their encouragement and counsel in our endeavors have
made this book possible.

Although our historical guide is perfectly intelligible and meaningful
read separately, it is meant to interface with these two volumes. The largest
number of references quoted is from them, those marked CHOC referring to
The Christian History of The Constitution of the United States of America,
and T&L referring to *Teaching and Learning America's Christian History*.

1. The Christian History of the Constitution of the United States of America: *Christian Self-Government.*

The landmark book on the Christian foundations of our nation. Traces
historically the Chain of Christianity moving westward to America. Exam-
ines the importance of The Bible as the "great political textbook." Documents the appearance, appreciation and application of Biblical principles of
government: how they were used to construct the American Christian republic. Compiled by Verna M. Hall. 450 pages, illustrated, excerpts & facsimiles
of actual historical documents, indexed. Bound in red vellum.

2. Teaching and Learning America's Christian History: The Principle Approach

Provides the keys to teaching Biblical principles of government from
Christian History (book #1) in all grades and subjects. Traces the subtle
subversion of America's Christian system of education by state-sponsored

humanism, makes clear the distinction between paganistic progressive education and Christian education. Charts, maps, Biblical index. Keyed to The Scriptures. A study course for adult and youth, home, church and school, by Rosalie J. Slater. Bound in red vellum, 400 pages.

Special Note:

Please order these two books from:

> The Foundation for American Christian Education
> P. O. Box 27035
> San Francisco, Ca. 94127

To receive the special study group price of $13.00 for both books, be sure to mention the book *The American Covenant – The Untold Story*.

Another valuable volume, the first edition of Noah Webster's *American Dictionary of the English Language,* published in 1828, is also available from the Foundation for American Christian Education in a facsimile edition, with an excellent biography of Webster by Rosalie J. Slater. (The price is $15.00.)

In *The American Covenant – The Untold Story* and its two companion volumes, the student has a basic library of America's history and important original documents.

The guide may be used effectively for:
– a self-study course in the origin and purpose of America.
– a family study course to train children in the art of self-government and for future leadership.
– an adult Bible study course or church school class.
– a semester course in the fundamental principles of American history and government for high school and college students.

Suggestions for Study

It is important that the student, after reading each chapter, take the time to gain an in-depth understanding of the subjects covered by completing the supplementary reading at the end of the chapter and testing their understanding by answering the questions. When the guide is used by study groups, the leader will find the questions provide a useful springboard for discussion of the principles learned and their application to contemporary problems.

Background of Publisher and its Institute

The Foundation for Christian Self-Government was founded in 1976 by Rev. Marshall Foster as a non-profit, non-denominational, educational foundation. Since that time, it has been committed to the education of the American people in the great principles of self- and civil government handed down to us from our Founding Fathers.

In 1982 the Foundation For Christian Self-Government launched the Mayflower Institute to teach America's Christian history to leaders in every field. The Institute is in voluntary association with several other foundations and thousands of individuals and has accepted the challenge to help restore our nation to its historic moorings. If you would like more copies of *The American Covenant*, further information on the 52-minute film of the same name, or a complete list of available materials for study, including study leader's guide and videotaped seminars, write:

Foundation for Christian Self-Government
P. O. Box 1087
Thousand Oaks, California 91360

Introduction

Most people in America today feel trapped in a slowly sinking ship. They see inflation and excessive taxation eating their incomes and their future dreams. They know they are losing their children to an educational system that turns out functional illiterates and fosters peer groups that destroy the character of their youth and the family structure. The majority of Americans questioned in the most extensive survey ever done of the American family, conducted by George Gallup in 1980, sense the growing hand of the state closing in on their political, economic, and religious liberty. But this same survey indicates that most Americans including Christians, although sensing the encroachment into their lives of government, nevertheless look to the federal government to remedy their loss of freedom, loss of economic prosperity, and their failure at childrearing.

How is it that our people have been fooled into entrusting their families, finances, and futures to an all-powerful state? Can it be that most Americans have been programmed to become government dependents? It appears so.

Most Christians who claim liberty from within through faith in Christ (John 8:36) and who are told in the Scriptures that they have internal dominion over sin (Romans 6:11), still find that in the reality of the external world their lives are out of control in a universe of economic chaos, political tyranny, and nuclear blackmail.

Is there a Biblical historically-proven method of dealing with this dilemma without accepting tyranny or waiting until the coming of Christ for victory over the forces that are engulfing us and our children?

The answer is emphatically – yes! Two thousand years ago our Lord unleashed upon the world the most powerful world-changing force ever known to man – the *self-governing Christian*. This new man, freed from the shackles of sin and guilt and armed with the only weapon that can subdue the earth and its institutions – the Word of God – became the bulwark of a movement that was begun by God Himself and about which Jesus said, *"the gates of hell shall not prevail against it"* (Matt. 16:18). Historically, whenever this new creation (the Christian) has understood God's instructions and has applied them to *all* spheres of life, he has gained dominion over his circumstances. He has progressively proven what *"whatsoever is born of God overcometh the world"* (I John 5:4). He is not dominated by history; he shapes it according to God's will.

It is important to clarify that we are not suggesting that this self-governing Christian, who received his greatest liberty in America, was of any one particular denomination, or nationality. Nor are we saying that the covenants of our forefathers with God put them in a "special nation" category impervious to divine judgment. Our reference to the American Covenant is no allusion to the theology of any particular denomination but is an attempt to highlight the historical significance of the various colonial covenants with God, which, when taken as a whole, became a great motivational, unifying and preserving influence upon our nation.

This study guide is written for the purpose of teaching students, parents, and individuals in all walks of life how they can be self-governing through God's power and Word in every area of life. We have placed this study in the context of America's Christian history because we, as Americans, have received the greatest heritage and example of Christian self-government ever known to man. Our founders built a nation based upon the premise that the self-governing Christians will produce the finest society. God blessed them as they trained their children in the art of self-government. Samuel Adams, October 4, 1790, summarized the type of training that produced the men who formed our nation:

> *"Let divines and philosophers, statesmen and patriots, unite their endeavors to renovate the age, by impressing the minds of men with the importance of educating their little boys and girls, of inculcating in the minds of youth the fear and love of the Deity and universal philanthropy, and, in subordination to these great principles, the love of their country; of instructing them in the art of self-government without which they never can act a wise part in the government of societies, great or small; in short, of leading them in the study and practice of the exalted virtues of the Christian system..."* (CHOC, p. XIV)

Our Founders' children grew up knowing the art of self-government and that art became the dominant factor in the forming of American culture. But today the Bible and Christianity have been pushed aside and Christians have become a counter-culture that has little effect upon our nation's power base. *The Wall Street Journal* recently discussed a growing movement of born-again Christians but minimized their impact because of their fragmentation on political and even moral issues.[1]

If we are to reverse the current humanistic dominance in our culture, we must understand how our Christian nation was undermined and what we must know and do if things are to be changed.

The Battle of Ideas

As you enter upon this study, it is essential that the vital nature and nation-changing capacity of your task be emphasized. The battle for control and leadership of the world has always been waged most effectively at the idea level. An idea, whether right or wrong, that captures the minds of a nation's youth will soon work its way into every area of society, especially in our multi-media age. *Ideas determine consequences*. Through the study of this guide and its companion volumes, individuals throughout our nation are discovering the missing links, the untold stories, and the forgotten principles that, if studied and applied, will result in a new reformation in our country. To illustrate the importance of ideas and the study of them for the changing of nations, let us briefly survey the rise of socialism in America. In only 30 years, the ideas of a small minority become the dominant philosophy in America's educational institutions and its political structure.

September 12, 1905

On the above date in the loft above Peck's restaurant at 140 Fulton Street in lower Manhattan, a group of young men met to plan the overthrow of the predominantly Christian world-view that still pervaded America. At this first meeting five men were present: Upton Sinclair, 27, a writer and a socialist; Jack London, writer; Thomas Wentworth Higginson, a unitarian minister; J.G. Phelps Stokes, husband of a socialist leader; and Clarence Darrow, a lawyer. Their organization was called the Intercollegiate Socialist Society. Their purpose was to "promote an intelligent interest in socialism among college men and women."[2] These men were ready to become the exponents of an idea passed on to them by an obscure writer named Karl Marx[3] – a man who never tried to be self-supporting but was supported by a wealthy industrialist who, inexplicably, believed in his theory of "the dictatorship of the proletariat." Although a small group in the beginning, these adherents of socialism more than succeeded in their task.

By using the proven method of *gradualism*, taken from the Roman general, Quintus Fabius Maximus, these men and others who joined with them slowly infiltrated their ideas onto the college campuses and into the public schools of our nation. By 1912 there were chapters in 44 colleges. By 1917 there were 61 chapters in schools and 12 in graduate schools. In 1921 they changed their name to the League for Industrial Democracy and entered the mainstream of America's education elite. By the mid-1930's there were 125 chapters of student study groups of the League for Industrial Democracy. At that time John Dewey, the godfather of progressive education, was the vice-president of the league. By 1941 Dewey had become president and Reinhold Niebuhr, the liberal socialist theologian, was the treasurer.[4]

Today, as a result of the efforts of a small minority of men who dared to study and propagate their ideas (no matter how abhorrent they were to the character of a Christian nation), their philosophy has become dominant in America's major cultural spheres. Now we, as American Christians, are fighting a counter-offense to recapture our nation. But the reason we find ourselves in this defensive position, is because we have abandoned our Biblical dominion mandate and the legacy given to us by our forefathers. As we begin our study, keep in mind that only a small group of men and women usually will dare to enter the idea field. Armed with the truth – the Bible and its application – and the examples of our Founding Fathers, lies and distortions must not defeat us. Let us set out then to take command of our world as our Founders once did that we, too, might be overcomers and more than conquerors through Christ.

Notes:

1. Jonathan Kaufman, "Old Time Religion, An Evangelical Revival Is Sweeping the Nation But with Little Effect," *Wall Street Journal* (July 11, 1980).
2. Paul W. Shafer and John Howland Snow, *The Turning of the Tides* (New Canaan, Connecticut: The Long House, Inc., 1962), p. 1.
3. See Robert Payne, *Marx, A Biography* (New York: Simon and Schuster, 1968).
4. Shafer and Snow, pp. 2-3.

Chapter 1

Clearing the Smokescreens

"For the weapons of our warfare are not carnal, but mighty through God to the pulling down of strongholds; Casting down imaginations and every high thing that exalteth itself against the knowledge of God, and bringing into captivity every thought to the obedience of Christ;"

II Corinthians 10:4,5

1

GEORGE WASHINGTON ADDRESSING THE CONSTITUTIONAL CONVENTION
(1787)
BY JUNIUS B. STEARNS

"Let us raise a standard to which the wise and honest can repair; the event is in the hand of God."

– George Washington

Chapter 1

Clearing the Smokescreens

The untold story of America's covenant relationship with God is once again being unveiled to the American people. This book is part of a renewal in understanding of what God did in the founding of our nation. It is a result of 25 years of historical research. The writers have not created a story or tried to fit Christianity and its God into American history. What they have uncovered is that this nation, its republican institutions, economic prosperity, and individual liberty can only be attributed to the hand of God and the covenant between our founders and their Creator.

For several generations we have been assured that the American experience is just the chance accumulation of adventurers, Deists, aristocrats, convicts and religious outcasts who came here seeking their own economic gain, seizing the Indians' land, using slaves to clear the forests, and stumbling into assured prosperity because of abundant natural resources. The above stereotype is portrayed in varying degrees through television dramas, history textbooks, and news commentaries.

Because the Providential perspective of this book is new to our generation, although certainly not to our Founders, we felt it was important to address common questions and doubts that hang as shadows over the possibility of restoring The American Covenant. In seminars throughout America, the authors have found that there are some basic questions that consistently recur. Let us begin to clear away the smokescreens of falsehood and ignorance that stand between us and the restoration of our republic.

Question #1
Why is our History so Important?

One of the premises of this study guide is that the recounting of the hand of God in the founding and preservation of our nation must of necessity be given great priority if there is to be hope for a cultural and spiritual restoration. The Bible clearly teaches that reformation cannot occur in a vacuum without historical reference. In the book of Deuteronomy a pattern is laid down for the renewal of a nation and its people. The pattern is repeated in both Testaments (see the sermons of the Apostles in the book of Acts) with variations, but it begins with the concept of *remembering* God's deeds in history. "Remember" is the key word in Deuteronomy, repeated frequently throughout the book as a command that was to begin the repentant process of rebuilding. Deuteronomy (second law) was the second statement of the Law to a new generation about to enter the Promised Land. Their fathers had died in the wilderness having forgotten God's Law and their covenant. Now a new generation needed to be reminded why they had fallen. God had long prepared their deliverance from Egypt and they were commanded to recount it and give God the glory.

Deuteronomy 5:15 says: "And remember that thou wast a servant in the land of Egypt, and that the Lord thy God brought thee out thence through a mighty hand and by a stretched out arm."

But the generation that Joshua led into the Promised Land soon forgot this admonition and in Judges 2:10 we read after the death of Joshua and the elders, "And there arose another generation after them which knew not the Lord, nor yet the works which he had done for Israel." As a result it goes on to say that they went off and worshipped the Baals and pluralized their faith in godless idolatry. Does this sound familiar?

Constantly, in addresses by the prophets, Apostles, and our Lord, we see the admonition to remember God's deeds and to recognize how they have abandoned His way. The major sermons of the Apostles quoted in the Book of Acts begin with an historical treatise on the falling away of God's people from His blessing (Acts 7). In Revelation 2:5 Jesus says to the church at Ephesus: "Nevertheless I have somewhat against thee, because thou hast left thy first love. Remember therefore from whence thou art fallen, and repent, and do the first works." Notice here that they had to *remember* even before they could *repent*.

We in the United States today have forgotten what God did for us. Many Americans would say that they do remember and acknowledge Christ as their personal liberator from the bondage of sin. But how many of us celebrate God's work in liberating us from 2500 years of domination under the totalitarian rule of the Divine Right of Kings? Since the time of Samuel the prophet in 1120 B.C. until the founding of this nation the pagan idea of man and government had dominated the world scene. But since the American Christian today does not know what God has done for him, is it any wonder that his personal repentance only works a personal reformation? For there to be a national reformation there must also be repentance for sins of omission and commission by the Christians who have forgotten the covenant of their fathers and the hand of God in our history.

Our Christian foundation and all of the godly institutions that were by-products of the Biblical faith of our forefathers, are to be passed on as a legacy and we, as Christians, are held accountable for what we do with this unprecedented heritage. Jesus said, "to whom much is given, much is required." We had better remember and recount God's history – His story – to our children and to a perishing generation or be prepared to lose our freedom.

Rev. S. W. Foljambe summarized the importance of our history on January 5, 1876 saying:

"The more thoroughly a nation deals with its history, the more decidedly will it recognize and own an overruling providence therein, and the more religious a nation will it become; while the more superficially it deals with its history seeing only secondary causes and agencies, the more irreligious will it be." (CHOC, p. Ia)

Verna M. Hall summarizes the way of restoration and its roots in historical remembrance in the introduction to *Christian History of the American Revolution*, page XXXV. She says:

"America from the days of creation has been for God's glory and for His people and if His people will be willing to learn what He has done for them in the days past, repent, and ask God's forgiveness for forgetting what He has done in bringing America into being, God will deal with her enemies within and without."

Is history important to study? It is so significant that the future of our Republic may well be determined by what we do with our great legacy.

Question #2
Why is America's Christian History Relevant to our Present Crisis?

A knowledge of America's Christian history makes it possible to discern fundamental answers to current problems in our nation. Many politically active Christians and media personalities are today addressing the issues of the day but most, unfortunately, have little knowledge of our history. Because of this lack of knowledge, many spokesmen become easy prey for well-trained humanist journalists who know all of the clichés about the "witch-hunts," the "bigoted Puritans" and the "blessings" of pluralism. While Christian leaders call for a return to a God-centered America, the well-entrenched secularist undermines the message by equating it with extremism and visions of the Ayatollah Khomeini or Jim Jones. If Christians do not know their true history, a false sense of guilt will set in and they will be placed on the defensive concerning their God and their country. Once in a defensive, reactionary position, the Christian community is one of the easiest groups in American to immobilize, because Christians who know the Bible know they cannot and should not force their beliefs on others. They do not want a church-run society and if they think this is the only option other than a secular, "do your own thing" state, they will complacently opt for the latter. The beauty of America's heritage is that our Founders provided the third alternative: a nation with true liberty and justice for *all*, including both the believer and the unbeliever.

Here are some specific examples of how a knowledge of America's Christian history clarifies issues and answers current dilemmas.

What is the Separation of Church and State?

This question is one of the hottest debates of the 1980's in the courts and legislative halls of our land. The term "separation of church and state" is used today as a catch-all phrase to eliminate religious influence upon anything involving the state or civil affairs. The history of the First Amendment to the Constitution gives us quite a different perspective. Our Founders had come from European lands ruled by monarchies which used official state churches to control the people. They had had enough of the supposed "divine right of kings." So, according to James Madison, the First Amendment was drawn up because "the people feared one sect might obtain a preeminence, or two combine together, and establish a religion to which they would compel others to conform."[1] The amendment was meant to shield the churches from the encroachment of the Federal Government, specifically, the Congress. But the framers of the Bill of Rights never intended that the church (speaking of the Christians and their various denominations) was to have no influence over the state or that religion was to be separated from our national life by an impregnable wall of separation.

Our Founding Fathers presupposed Christianity as the moral foundation of governmental action. George Washington said: "True religion offers the government its surest support."[2] Supreme Court Justice Joseph Story, writing in the early days of the republic, said of the period when the First Amendment was adopted: "An attempt to level all religions, and to make it a matter of state policy to hold all in utter indifference, would have created universal disapprobation, if not universal indignation...."[3] He explained further that the real object of the amendment was "to prevent any national ecclesiastical establishment which should give to a hierarchy the exclusive patronage of the national government."[4]

In 1849, Robert C. Winthrop stated the common understanding of the Constitutional period well when he said:

"It may do for other countries, and other governments to talk about the State supporting religion. Here, under our own free institutions, it is Religion which must support the State."[5]

What then has caused the present discordant division between religion and the state? The term "separation of church and state" is not in the First Amendment or, indeed, anywhere in the Constitution. It appears in a personal letter Thomas Jefferson wrote in 1802 replying to one from a group of Baptists and Congregationalists in Danbury, Connecticut questioning his religious position. (As a matter of fact, Jefferson was neither a member of the Constitutional Convention of 1787, nor of the first Congress under the Constitution which passed the Bill of Rights.) Yet the Supreme Court has consistently relied on this personal statement by a man who had nothing to do with writing the Bill of Rights to uphold their rulings that public schools may not hold devotional exercises or Bible readings, that the Ten Commandments may not be posted on the walls of schoolrooms, and many other anti-religious decisions.

In view of the foregoing, it is well to remind ourselves of what the First Amendment actually says: "Congress shall make no law respecting an establishment of religion, or prohibiting the free exercise thereof..." John W. Whitehead, a respected Constitutional lawyer and author, gives the following excellent paraphrase of the Amendment into modern English: "The federal government shall make no law having anything to do with supporting a national denominational church, or prohibiting the free exercise of religion."[6]

Surely the mass of historical evidence from which we have quoted makes it clear that "separation of church and state," is a non-Constitutional phrase now used as a battle-cry by those who would frighten godly Americans out of the polls and back to the pews and is a blatant distortion of the intent of the Framers of the First Amendment.

Education in the Light of History

No greater issue looms in the minds of American parents than that of the failure of the American educational system. This failure can best be analyzed from the perspective of America's Christian history focusing on the long-term reasons for the demise of education in America. Otherwise, the debate becomes an existential "blame sharing" match between teachers, parents, and bureaucrats crying for more money.

We must see the comparison and contrast between the historic educational philosophy of early America versus the modern, progressive methodology and content used in most schools today if we hope to have a reference point or standard by which to judge and change the present educational establishment.

Early American Education

Early education in America was unique, as it was founded upon private education in the home, churches, and schools with the Bible as the foundation stone for character development as well as intellectual insight. The Pilgrims and Puritans were greatly interested in education, but they saw it as a personal, family, and church responsibility. Sometimes formal education was offered at the township level, but always under parental control and Biblically-based. These early founders, knowing the importance of education, founded hundreds of private schools and colleges during the colonial period. Most of the colleges were started in order to train men for the ministry. Rosalie J. Slater gives this documentation on the fruit of our Founder's educational efforts:

> "*At the time of the* Declaration of Independence *the quality of education had enabled the colonies to achieve a degree of* literacy from 70% to virtually 100%. *This was not education restricted to the few. Modern scholarship reports 'the prevalence of schooling and its accessiblity to all segments of the population.' Moses Coit Tyler, historian of American*

literature, indicates the colonists' 'familiarity with history...extensive legal learning...lucid exposition of constitutional principles, showing, indeed, that somehow, out into the American wilderness had been carried the very accent of cosmopolitan thought and speech.' When the American State Papers arrived in Europe...they were found to contain 'nearly every quality indicative of personal and national greatness.'" (T&L, p. 89)

In tracing the greatness of our nation, no more important foundation can be found than the 150 years of tutelage in the Christian schools and the self-governing, principled study and reasoning done in the homes by rich and poor alike.

Because all education was built upon the foundation of the Bible, students grew up knowing how to reason from its principles to *all* of human endeavor. The Bible was the political and economic textbook of the patriots. Rev. J. Wingate Thornton's *Pulpit of the American Revolution* notes that in 1777 the Continental Congress wrote "directing the Committee of Commerce to import twenty thousand copies of the Bible, the great political textbook of the patriots..." (CHOC, p. 375)

Modern Progressive Education

In 1838, Horace Mann became the Secretary of the Massachusetts Board of Education. Did you know that during the following years, Mann promoted a philosophy of education that was diametrically opposed to that of the Founding Father generation? He is known as the father of the public school movement.

1. He supported forced taxation for state schools which undermined parental control and was detrimental to the private schools.
2. Mann, and those who followed him, de-emphasized the Biblical doctrine of salvation as the basis of character development, replacing it with the optimistic, humanistic view of the perfectibility of man through education and environment.
3. He encouraged group thinking and study rather than individual initiative and creativity.
4. He standardized teacher training, textbooks, and accreditation beginning the transition away from the principles of the Christian philosophy of education taught by the great founder of America's educational system, Noah Webster.[7]

As the twentieth century dawned, John Dewey, with his progressive method of education, derived partially from his exposure to the Communist educational system in Russia, carried on the death march toward federal secularism. By 1935, a man-centered curriculum had become the dominant influence in most fields of scholarship in this country.

The public school bureaucracy, which is now the largest in the history of the world, has been "vaccinating" the vast majority of America's youth for several generations against what it considers to be "the infectious disease of absolute moral values," our Christian heritage, and our Christian republic which was built upon these truths.

Today, as progressive, public education collapses before our eyes, damaging millions of young lives in the process, we are witnessing an inevitable consequence of 150 years which cannot be corrected by simply putting voluntary (pluralistic) prayers back in the schools. A complete change of philosophy and leadership is needed.

Through a knowledge of America's Christian history, not only can the progressive public school be exposed, but the positive alternative of the "Principle Approach" to education used in early America be instituted in its place. Criticizing the status quo is an American past-time, but the real question is: How many of us will be willing to sacrifice our time and private funds to rebuild and not tear down? Learning the deeds of our Fathers will not only cause us to repent but will give us the wisdom needed to restore the broken down walls of our culture.

Summary

Other questions such as the reason for the rise in crime, the failure of the government control of welfare, the failure of the jurisprudence system, the failure of evangelical activity to transform society, the dramatic drop in the productivity of our economy, and the jump in inflation can all be understood only when placed against the backdrop of our history and an examination of Scripture. Let us not lose our future by failing to come to grips with our past. We, like the church at Ephesus in Revelation 2, need to repent and do the deeds we did at first; but first we must learn what those deeds were!

Question #3
Is There Time to Restore America?
Isn't Evangelism More Urgent?

First, let us say that there is no greater priority than world evangelism. Our Founders would agree with that statement and, in fact, many of them were fundamentally motivated by this goal as they came to America. William Bradford, the Pilgrim historian and governor, clearly stated that the Pilgrims came with a desire to spread the gospel worldwide when they covenanted with God to found their colony:

> "...a great hope and inward zeall they had of laying some good foundation, or at least to make some way therunto, for ye propagating and advancing ye gospell of ye kingdom of Christ in those remote parts of ye world; yea, though they should be but even as stepping-stones unto others for ye performing of so great a work." (CHOC p. 193)

Presupposing the above priority to "disciple the nations" (Matt. 28:18-20) and to "preach the gospel to every creature" (Mark 16:15), it is important to keep in mind that God is glorified and people reached not only through *words* but by His children *showing* the practical application of Christianity to all of life. Nowhere has the balance between evangelism and the manifestation of Christianity in culture been so clearly illustrated as in America. Our nation came into being through the obedience of millions of Christians who took God's gospel and its application into *every sphere of life*. When we were caring for our own vineyard we were likened to a "city on a hill" and a "light to the nations" showing forth the power of Christ in the life of individuals manifest on a corporate scale.

Is There Time to Occupy?

Over the past 140 years or so there has been a growing trend among many religious groups to speculate on the exact date of the end of the world and the second coming of Christ. Many people have been led to faith in Christ as a result of studying the coming of Christ in judgment at the end of time. But the setting of dates concerning His return and over-speculation as to the significance of current events in relation to this subject sometimes have caused many to lose hope of reformation of our government and society.

The purpose of this book is not to critique or take sides on eschatological issues. But one point should be clearly made concerning our attitude toward

11

Christ's return regardless of what millenial view we have. We, as Christians, will not be judged on how well we guessed the exact time of Christ's coming, but concerning the deeds we have done to build His Kingdom while He is not physically present (Luke 19, II Cor. 5:10). Regardless of when Jesus Christ comes again, and only the Father knows the time (Acts 1:7), Christians cannot ignore their stewardship to "occupy until I come" (Luke 19:13). Who and what will occupy and thereby govern and control the quality and conduct of our nation and its administration as well as our homes, churches, and schools? The Christian or the unbeliever? Which group of people was given the commission to occupy? Who has taken leadership in our society – Christians or unbelievers? Will Biblical principles occupy only our Christian homes, churches, and missionary endeavors and not the civil, economic, or cultural spheres of life in America because there is not time? Or because there is no vision or faith to labor? A knowledge of God's hand in American history assures us that God gives His people the time needed to accomplish what He has called them to do."Righteousness exalts a nation, but sin is a reproach to any people." (Prov. 14:34)

"If the Foundations be Destroyed"

Consider the consequences for the world if America should succumb to humanism and socialism. What would be the dreadful fate of other men and nations if this fountainhead of evangelical Christianity spurned God? For America is the one nation with the liberty, property, and form of government capable of protecting, not crushing, the voluntary expression of the Gospel of Jesus Christ. We need look no further than behind the Iron and Bamboo Curtains to find the answer.

God's Power in Building a Nation

Today many of our missionaries are scorned as they present the Gospel in foreign lands. Nationals from various countries rightly ask the question, "If your Christ is so powerful that He can save my soul, can He do nothing for my nation? What has He done for *your* nation, America?" Unfortunately, many of our missionaries are not taught the answer to that question. As a result the great Scriptural principles of nation-building that could result in a national reformation in these lands are not imparted from the Word of God and our Christian history. But Christ and His Word do offer liberty, not only from the burden of personal sin, but also *from external tyranny* when His sovereignty is acknowledged by the people of a nation and His Word is heeded (Proverbs 29:2). The people of the world need to know that Communism cannot hold a candle to our world-changing God and His people in any field of human endeavor, and that history proves this out. They also need to see a model again of a reformed America. We cannot cut the Gospel message away from its external manifestations. Isaiah 58:12 is vital today: "They that shall be of thee shall build the old waste places: thou shalt *raise up the foundations of many generations;* and thou shalt be called, the *repairer* of the breech, the *restorer* of the paths to dwell in."

Question #4
Don't Spiritual Activities Take Priority Over Secular Pursuits?

We Americans have been taught in the last few generations that there is a separation between the spiritual and secular pursuits of life. In the 1950's religion was defined as a personal thing, the implication being "don't talk about it or try to push it into other 'non-religious' areas of life." But the question must be asked: "Are there any non-religious areas of life?"

I was speaking to a large audience of pastors recently concerning the strategic need to rebuild our nation to the glory of God. After my address a pastor from Southern California came up to me and said, "What you are attempting to do is a worthy effort. But, ultimately you know, if God wants to restore our nation, He will do it. All we can do is pray." I paused and asked him if he had any farmers in his church and he said he did. I said, "Why don't we go back to our churches and tell our farmers not to plant their spring crops, but to simply pray and believe; if it is God's will, we will have a great harvest in the fall." The pastor got the point. Prayer is important, but if we do not sow our seeds into every area of life, we will have no harvest to reap but the destruction of our liberty and the rise of totalitarianism.

The philosophy mentioned above must be traced back to the Greek philosophers who separated physical life from the aesthetic or spiritual life. The Catholic theologian, Thomas Aquinas, expounded the view that there was an area of life called "grace" in the realm of the spiritual, and a separate, autonomous area called "nature" in the realm of natural activities or wordly pursuits (see Francis Schaeffer's *Escape From Reason* for further details). The implications of this philosophy are that God is needed to understand the spiritual but that our human reason is adequate to direct most human activities. The philosophers of the Enlightenment expanded this concept. Now, in the twentieth century, many unbelievers see no need for the spiritual element whatsoever since they see themselves as evolved animals with no soul or eternal destiny. Many believers, on the other hand, have little use for "earthly affairs" since they view all but "religious" activity as secular.

In recent years there has been a great revival of Biblical Christianity. Some good results from the development have occurred, including an emphasis on the need for a personal relationship with Jesus Christ but, unfortunately, the negative of this movement has been the classification of certain activities as "spiritual" and others as "secular."

Preaching Politics?

A great Colonial pastor was confronted by this same attitude prior to the War of Independence, although in those days it was held by a small minority. When Jonathan Mayhew, a Congregational minister at West Church, Boston, heard of the English Parliament's plan to impose the Episcopal Church on America as its State Church, he was aroused to vigorous opposition. Around him, men's hearts were filled with consternation. Had not their forefathers fled to New England to escape persecution by the State Church which had thrown ministers and laymen alike into foul prisons, there to rot and die? What could they do? Some Colonial ministers preached blind submission to the higher powers, but Mayhew was outraged at such teaching. Feelings in Boston were running high when he mounted his pulpit and preached the sermon that became famous throughout the colonies and was even read with anger in far-off London.

In this sermon, "Concerning Unlimited Submission to the Higher Powers," he attacks such submission head-on. "It is evident that the *affairs of civil government* may properly *fall under a moral and religious consideration*...For, although there be a sense, and a very plain and important sense, in which Christ's Kingdom is not of this world, His inspired apostles have nevertheless, laid down some general principles concerning the office of civil rulers, and the duty of subjects, together with the reason and obligation of that duty. And...it is proper for all who acknowledge the authority of Jesus Christ, and the inspiration of His apostles, to endeavor to understand what is in fact the doctrine which they have delivered concerning this matter." (CHOC, p. 375)

And not only this matter! For when the sermon was published later by popular demand, Mayhew commented in his preface tht he hoped few people would think the subject an improper one "under a notion that this is *preaching politics* instead of Christ...I beg it may be remembered that 'all Scripture is profitable for doctrine, for reproof, for correction, for instruction in righteousness.' Why, then, should not those parts of Scripture which relate to *civil government* be examined and explained from the desk, as well as others?" (CHOC, p. 374)

Why not, indeed? Why not take the Scriptures and apply them to all areas of our lives? Mayhew's words are an eloquent answer today to the false division that would split our lives into two mutually exclusive areas: the religious and the secular.

No Neutrality

At last it appears that millions of Americans are remembering the great truths of the Reformation, such as the priesthood of all believers (emphasizing the importance of the individual) and the sovereignty of God over every sphere of life. There is no neutral (or secular) area of life. When we set up an area or institution not acknowledging God's sovereignty we become an enemy of God and are in rebellion. The public school system in America is a good example. It is not neutral religiously. It has simply exchanged the Christian religion for that of humanism.

It should be noted that in 1961 in the Torasco vs. Watkins case, the Supreme Court recognized secular humanism as a religion. In delivering the unanimous opinion, Justice Hugo Black stated: "Among religions in this country which do not teach what would generally be considered a belief in the existence of God are Buddhism, Taoism, Ethical Culture, Secular Humanism, and others."[8]

The Biblical World-View

The Biblical world-view demands that all human endeavor be a service to God, whether praying or riveting together a plane. Men's vocations, therefore, are holy callings just as are church work or missionary activity. In Genesis, when the descendants of Adam are named, their occupations are also given. (Gen. 4:20-22) When all of life is seen in this context, then important "spiritual" exercises, such as prayer, Bible study, and fellowship with fellow believers, take on greater importance in our battle for the whole world, both physical and spiritual. In light of our current crisis, nothing could be more spiritual than saving our children from humanism, our economy from deprivation, and our liberty from extinction.

Question #5

Weren't We Founded by Deists, Unruly Adventurers, and Religions Castaways?

This stereotype presented in TV docu-dramas and history classrooms throughout the nation is one of the greatest defamations of national character ever perpetrated upon a people.

The influence of Deism in America was minimal until the nineteenth century when it made inroads through the Unitarian Church and the atheistic philosophy of the French Revolution. During our Founding period, however, it had little influence. According to historian Perry Miller, Deism was strictly "an exotic plant" imported from Europe which did not flourish here. This distinguished historian also makes the point that the colonial clergy presented to the people a religious rationale for the American Revolution which united them behind its goals.[9] Deism was incapable of producing such a phenomenon. It professed a belief in one God but denied the divine origin of Scriptures. Its weak philosophy of a non-active, spectator God who left all of the affairs of the world to human whim was no match for the powerful Biblical faith of the majority of our people in the Founding Father generation.

Even Jefferson and Franklin, the two men most often quoted as being Deists, give little credence to the view in their writings. Undoubtedly, both of these men did imbibe a mixture of European religious heresies, but the predominant influence upon their world continued to be Christian.

Franklin's Plea for Public Prayer

In the summer of 1787 a feeling of desperation and deadlock had descended upon the Constitutional Convention. Men from various states were planning to leave and it would be years before they could gather again for another try at bringing the loosely-knit confederated colonies together to form a republic.

On June 28, 1787, as the Convention was ready to adjourn in dissension, a wise old man addressed its President, George Washington, with quiet simplicity:

"How has it happened, Sir, that we have not hitherto once thought of humbly appealing to the Father of lights to illuminate our understandings? In the beginning of the contest with Great Britain, when we were sensible to danger, we had daily prayers in this room for Divine protection. Our prayers, Sir, were heard and they were graciously

16

answered....I have lived, Sir, a long time and the longer I live, the more
convincing proofs I see of this truth — that God governs in the affairs of
men. – And if a sparrow cannot fall to the ground without His notice, is
it probable that an empire can rise without His aid? We have been as-
sured, Sir, in the sacred writings that 'except the Lord build the house,
they labor in vain that build it.'...I firmly believe this..."[10]

Benjamin Franklin's words were heeded and the Convention went on to complete its task. Although Franklin is often classified as a Deist, it is clear from the above statements that he had been deeply influenced by the Christian world-view and such great Christian ministers as George Whitefield.

It could well be argued that many Christians today have acted more like Deists than the few men accused of this heresy in our founding, because today we often give lip-service to the Lord Jesus Christ over all things, but then act as though He were an absentee, distant monarch just biding His time to claim His throne!

Don't Believe What You See

Regarding the charge that wild adventurers and womanizers roamed the land in early America, there is little need for refutation. On the frontier, starting in the times of the Puritans, some scouts and settlers did precede the church and families, and there were some atrocities perpetrated upon the Indians and some rowdy settlements. But as soon as settlements were established and churches were formed, the immoral and rowdy were made subject to the rule of law. The Christian women of the community, especially, demanded it. Our TV generation has absorbed too much western cowboy-fever, most of it fictitious distortions of true life in early America. The *US News and World Report* (May 21, 1979) reports that the American people receive most of their knowledge of history from watching TV docu-dramas. And most of these docu-dramas bear little resemblance to the true story of our history. Only by going back and reading the original documents, as you are going to be challenged to do in this study of America's Christian History, can you determine the real story.

The truth is that those who had saved their money and possessed the fortitude to settle this country were for the most part character-filled Christians. Rev. R.J. Rushdoony points out that it took two year's living expenses just to cross and settle America and that the well-established families with the Puritan work ethic and Christian faith were the true hardy breed that settled our country. These godly men and women, due to their family orientation, free-enterprise spirit, and Christian discipline, maintained cultural dominion over the sin-loving reprobates that we read so much about. Our history is evidence of the fact that, in the long-run, nothing can thwart an individual who has an understanding of his Commission from God to subdue the earth and who believes God for the victory.

Question #6
Was America Founded as a Christian Nation?

The question of our Biblical origins has been bandied around in intellectual circles for many years, especially now that there is a renewed Christian involvement in the culture of America. The major hurdle in answering the question is to define terms properly. The concept of a Christian nation is often written off because of misconceptions as to what this means. A Christian nation is not one in which all people in a society are Christians, just as in an Islamic country, not all people are necessarily Moslems. But in a Christian nation, as our Founders would have defined it, the principles and institutional foundations are Biblically based and the people in general share a Biblical world-view.

Nor should we confuse the term "Christian nation" with a "Christian state." Since the word state refers to a political body or the body politic of the nation, the term "Christian state" would mean one in which the government ruled in religious matters through a state church. This would, of course, preclude religious liberty.

All Laws Are a Codification of a Religious System

Nevertheless, it is imperative to understand that all laws of a nation are the codification of a presuppositional world-view, i.e., the laws of the United States have presupposed from the beginning that the Bible was the foundation of our system. Rev. John Wingate Thornton said:

> *"The highest glory of the American Revolution, said John Quincy Adams, was this: it connected in one indissoluble bond, the principles of civil government with the principles of Christianity." (CHOC, p. 372)*

Rev. Thornton's words condense and paraphrase comments Adams made in a July 4, 1837 oration, which are even more powerful in their full statement:

> *"Is it not that, in the chain of events, the birthday of the nation is in-*

dissolubly linked with the birthday of the Saviour? That it forms a leading event in the progress of the Gospel dispensation? Is it not that the Declaration of Independence first organized the social compact on the foundation of the Redeemer's mission? That it laid the cornerstone of human government upon the first precepts of Christianity and gave to the world the first irrevocable pledge of the fulfillment of the prophecies announced directly from Heaven at the birth of the Saviour and predicted by the greatest of the Hebrew prophets 600 years before?"[11]

Such convictions as these concerning the Christian foundations of our government persisted into comparatively recent times. John W. Whitehead analyzes the Supreme Court's historic understanding of the relationship between Christianity and government in the United States:

"In 1892 the United States Supreme Court made an exhaustive study of the supposed connection between Christianity and the government of the United States. After researching hundreds of volumes of historical documents, the Court asserted 'these references add a volume of unofficial declarations to the mass of organic utterances that this is a religious people...a Christian nation.' Likewise in 1931, Supreme Court Justice George Sutherland reviewed the 1892 decision in relation to another case and reiterated that Americans are a 'Christian people' and in 1952 Justice William O. Douglas affirmed 'we are a religious people and our institutions presuppose a Supreme Being.'"[12]

Christianity the Dominant Influence in America

America was under the dominant influence of Biblical Christianity from 1620 until well into the nineteenth century. There are many who, in their desire to lay claim to the great accomplishments of that era, have tried to minimize the Christian influence and take the credit for themselves. But only God deserves the glory for what He did in the founding of this great nation.

People from many denominations came to America in the early years, but the vast majority of them shared a common faith in the basic tenets of Christianity. Whitehead's research reveals that

"when the Constitution was adopted and sent to the States for ratification, the population of America numbered only about 3¼ million. The Christian population numbered at least 2 million. James C. Hefley has commented that about 900,000 were Scotch or Scotch-Irish Presbyteri-

ans, with another million also holding to basic Calvinistic beliefs."[13]

Christian Nation in Apostasy

It must be admitted that today, although we are still essentially a Christian nation in form (i.e., the Constitution, legal structure, church affiliation), we are not one in conduct. For the first 250 years of our existence Christian character determined the conduct of self-government in homes, churches, and civil society. But today we have forgotten our heritage and only the skeleton remains. Even so, deep within the American character there lingers a Christian conscience ready to be revived by the spirit of God through awakened American Christian patriots.

It should be noted that by stating that America was a Christian nation we are not saying that we were the "New Israel" or a special race that God must bless. Quite the contrary, God blessed America because our forefathers built their nation with reliance on Him and His Word, and because God had a Gospel purpose for our nation. If we turn from His purpose we can expect His judgment, perhaps greater judgment than other nations because "to whom much is given, much is required." (Luke 12:48)

Every nation can be a nation under God if it chooses to follow Jesus Christ (Psalm 2:10-12). Our history is unique in that we were allowed to express the full flower of Christian civilization and government. This fact should give us cause to ponder the price we have paid for the maintenance of our Christian liberty. Will we be the generation that presides over its death?

Question #7
Isn't it Better to Live in a Pluralistic Society Rather Than a Christian Nation?

The question above can be answered only if we come to grips with the myth of the greatness of the pluralistic society. Many Christians today have been taught that it is good to live in a "do your own thing" society where "anything goes" because that protects their liberty to worship and preach the Gospel. The argument goes like this: "I'll protect your right to sell pornographic literature and movies as long as you will let me preach Jesus."

The Counter Culture Blues

Barbara Morris in her book, *Change Agents in the Schools*, points to the fact that the public schools have become *values changers*, not just tools of education. In "values clarification" classes students are taught that there are no more absolutes in our "evolutionary," pluralistic world. For example, our children are taught that while we may not think it is right to kill grandmothers "by cultural consensus" (at least not yet), it may be fine for some cultures which have practiced it as a way of life for centuries. That is the type of reasoning used.

Oftentimes the Christian who finds the philosophy of relativism personally offensive gives in to it culturally because he has been conditioned by his education to accept the non-Christian culture as the norm. To complicate the problem, many Christians in the twentieth century have been taught that the world (God's created world) is evil and under the control of Satan. We, as Christians, are relegated to the status of misfits who can only hope to be a counter-culture. As a result of this attitude, many Christians pre-suppose the impossibility of a Christian nation because they believe the above distortions. The Bible teaches the opposite to be true.

Every nation is called upon to obey Jesus Christ (Psalm 2:10-12):

"Be wise now therefore, O ye kings: be instructed, ye judges of the earth. Serve the Lord with fear, and rejoice with trembling. Kiss the Son, lest he be angry, and ye perish from the way, when his wrath is kindled but a little. Blessed are all they that put their trust in him."

This is not a call to build pluralistic societies but godly ones which become disciples of our Lord: in other words, Christian nations.

In fact, in the Great Commission in Matthew 28:18-20 where we are given our marching orders, Jesus calls us to teach (make disciples of) the nations, teaching them to obey all that He has commanded.

There is no neutrality with God. Either a nation will be built upon a foundation of God's Word or it will be destroyed by "kindling the Son's wrath." A pluralistic society is just another term for a Christian nation that is on its way to becoming a humanistic society devoted to war with the Gospel. English historian E.R. Norman has observed:

"pluralism is a word society employs during the transition from one orthodoxy to another" (Imprimis, April 1981).

Whether you are Christian or not, as you read this study guide, consider this warning: If we abandon our Biblical roots for pluralism, we will soon lose all the attending benefits of Christian civilization such as law, absolute moral standards, a sound economy, a limited government, and any vestige of liberty that we still maintain.

The restoration of our land will not be accomplished by bartering with the devil for equal time. We must lead our society through the strength of our character, our Biblical reasoning and action, and our financial resources if there is to be liberty for either the righteous or the unrighteous. Proverbs 29:2 says that "when the righteous are in authority, the people rejoice: when the wicked beareth rule, the people mourn." As Christians we cannot hide behind the excuse that Satan rules the day, because he does not. We must work to restore our Republic which rightly belongs to God, not the devil. Unbelievers also should come to grips with the facts of history which show that only in a Christian Republic will their liberty of conscience be guaranteed. Pluralism, on the other hand, will lead us to tyranny. For its chaos of relative values leading to anarchy will ultimately succumb to some form of tyranny.

Some will say, "don't we have greater liberty today under pluralism?" Not true! Our founders would stand on another Lexington Green if they were here today and saw us submitting to 40% confiscation of our property through government taxes, the murder of 15 million babies through abortion taking from them their lives and liberty, and the State propagandizing the youth of our nation in the religion of secular humanism while forcing the Bible and prayer to be taken from our schools. We are not truly free today. Worse is coming if we do not restore our Christian nation through rebuilding the character of the American Christian.

Dr. Jedediah Morse, on April 25, 1799, summarized the decision that we face today:

> "To the kindly influence of Christianity we owe that degree of civil freedom and political and social happiness which mankind now enjoys. In proportion as the genuine effects of Christianity are diminished in any nation, either through unbelief, or the corruption of its doctrines, or the neglect of its institutions; in the same proportion will the people of that nation recede from the blessings of genuine freedom, and approximate the miseries of complete despotism." (CHOC, p. V)

The following statement by the eminent professor and theologian, Charles Hodge, Princeton Seminary, in 1876, illustrates the cogent and balanced thinking that once prevailed concerning our nation and its purpose. If we are to restore our nation, we must heed the words of men such as Rev. Hodge:

"The proposition that the United States of America are a Christian and Protestant nation, is not so much the assertion of a principle as the statement of a fact. That fact is not simply that the great majority of the people are Christians and Protestants, but that the organic life, the institutions, laws, and official action of the government, whether that action be legislative, judicial, or executive, is, and of right should be, and in fact must be, in accordance with the principles of Protestant Christianity.

"When Protestant Christians came to this country they possessed and subdued the land. They worshipped God, and his Son Jesus Christ as the Saviour of the World, and acknowledged the Scriptures to be the rule of their faith and practice. They introduced their religion into their families, their schools, and their colleges. They abstained from all ordinary business on the Lord's Day, and devoted it to religion. They built churches, erected school-houses, and taught their children to read the Bible and to receive and obey it as the Word of God. They formed themselves as Christians into municipal and state organizations. They acknowledged God in their legislative assemblies. They prescribed oaths to be taken in his name. They closed their courts, their places of business, their legislatures, and all places under the public control, on the Lord's Day. They declared Christianity to be part of the common law of the land. In the process of time thousands have come among us, who are neither Protestants nor Christians...All are welcomed; all are admitted to equal rights and privileges. All are allowed to acquire property, and to vote in every election, made eligible to all offices, and invested with equal influence in all public affairs. All are allowed to worship as they please, or not to worship at all, if they see fit. No man is molested for his religion or for his want of religion. No man is required to profess any form of faith, or to join any religious association. More than this cannot reasonably be demanded. More, however, is demanded. The infidel demands that the government should be conducted on the principle that Christianity is false. The atheist demands that it should be conducted on the assumption that there is no God, and the positivist on the principle that men are not free agents. The sufficient answer to all this is that it cannot possibly be done."[14]

Notes:

1. Jonathan Elliot, *The Debates of the Several State Conventions on the Adoption of the Federal Constitution*, Vol. 3, p. 45, quoted in John W. Whitehead, *The Second American Revolution* (Elgin, Ill.: David C. Cook Publishing Co., 1982), p. 96.
2. Verna M. Hall, comp., *The Christian History of the Constitution of the United States of America: Christian Self-Government with Union* (San Francisco: Foundation for American Christian Education, 1979), p. 68.
3. Joseph Story, *Commentaries on the Constitution of the United States*, Vol. 2, pp. 593-95, quoted in Whitehead, *The Second American Revolution*, p. 98.
4. Ibid.
5. Hall, *Christian History of the American Revolution*, p. 20.
6. John W. Whitehead, *The Separation Illusion* (Milford, Michigan: Mott Media, 1977), p. 90.
7. For further information on Horace Mann's approach to education, read his *Education of Free Men*.
8. See Tim La Haye, *The Battle for the Mind* (Old Tappan, New Jersey: Fleming H. Revell Company, 1980), p. 128.
9. See Perry Miller quotation from *Nature's God* in Francis A. Schaeffer, *A Christian Manifesto* (Westchester, Ill.: Crossway Books, 1981), pp. 128-29.
10. Issac A. Cornelison, *The Relation of Religion to Civil Government in the United States of America, a State Without a Church, but Not Without a Religion* (New York and London: G. P. Putnam and Sons, 1895), pp. 209-210.
11. John Quincy Adams, July 4, 1837 oration on the 61st anniversary of the Declaration of Independence (Newburyport, Mass.: Charles Whipple, 1837).
12. Foundation for Christian Self-Government, *Newsletter*, April 1981.
13. Ibid.
14. Charles Hodge, *Systematic Theology*, 1871, quoted in Hall, *Christian History of the American Revolution*, pp. 156-57.

Further Reading – Chapter 1

The Christian History of the Constitution of the United States of America (CHOC):

Teaching and Learning America's Christian History (T&L):

Questions

1.   Why is remembering our past important to our future? _____
_____
_____

2.   Why does God hold us accountable for what we do with our heritage of liberty? _____
_____
_____

3.   Did the Founding Fathers intend to separate religion from the state? ___
_____
_____

4.   What was the foundation stone of our educational system in America until 1838? _____
_____
_____

5.   What is the nature of the educational system that supplanted it? _____
_____
_____

6.   Why is "progressive" education really retrogressive? _____
_____
_____

7.   Why are Christian schools of vital importance for our children and the nation? _____
_____
_____

8. Shouldn't transformed Christians also transform the society around them? _____
_____
_____

9. Is it wrong to apply Christianity to "non-religious" areas of life? _____
_____
_____

10. Why did Colonial ministers preach on political as well as personal questions? _____
_____
_____

11. What traits of Christian character were vital in settling America? _____
_____
_____

12. What three elements are essential in order to restore America? _____
_____
_____

13. Why is it impossible to build a neutral nation without religious roots? _
_____
_____

Chapter 2

What Your History Books Never Told You

"For he established a testimony in Jacob, and appointed a law in Israel, which he commanded our fathers, that they should make them known to their children: that the generation to come might know them, even the children which should be born; who should arise and declare them to their children: that they might set their hope in God, and not forget the works of God, but keep his commandments: and might not be as their fathers, a stubborn and rebellious generation; a generation that set not their heart aright, and whose spirit was not steadfast with God."

Psalms 78:5-8

"A SPECIAL INSTRUMENT SENT OF GOD"

"About the 16th of March [1621], a certain Indian came boldly amongst them and spoke to them in broken English...His name was Samoset. He told them also of another Indian whose name was Squanto, a native of this place, who had been in England and could speak better English than himself...[A]bout four or five days after, came...the aforesaid Squanto....[He] continued with them and was their interpreter and was a special instrument sent of God for their good beyond their expectation."

–William Bradford
Of Plymouth Plantation

Chapter 2

What Your History Books Never Told You

The story that is revealed through a study of the original documents of our founders has within it a consistent reference to their faith in the Providential hand of God in the founding of their nation. Yet in the vast majority of modern textbooks on American history this central truth goes unrecognized. The above distortion or oversight, depending upon your perspective, has had a deadly impact upon the American republic and its youth. Walter Karp, writing in "Harpers," May 1980, p. 80, in an article entitled "Textbook America" states:

> "From the new textbooks, the children of the American republic will never gain knowledge of, or the slightest incentive to participate in, public affairs...No reader of these degraded texts will ever learn from them how to 'judge for themselves what will secure or endanger their freedom.' The new textbooks have snuffed out the very idea of human freedom, for that freedom at bottom is precisely the human capacity for action that political history records and that the textbooks are at such pains to conceal...What the political history of the textbooks reveals is that a powerful few, gaining control of public education, have been depriving the American republic of citizens, and popular government of a people to defend it. And the American history textbook, so innocent-seeming and inconsequential, has been their well-chosen instrument."

No Neutrality

The authors of this book and its accompanying volumes clearly admit that our interpretation of history presupposes that the God of the Bible controls history, intervenes through Providential events, and is bringing all events to a conclusion to show forth His glory.

Most modern educators, such as those who are responsible for the historical distortion spoken of previously, deny the Providential view of history and would have us believe that their promotion of one of several "secular" views of history is simply the recounting of brute facts. They fail to tell their students that their own humanist presuppositions and religious doctrines determine their choice and interpretation of people, places, principles, and events. They fail to communicate that there is no neutrality possible in the teaching of history, for the historian's world-view will dictate his perspective. Here again, Walter Karp's insight in "Harper's" magazine is of interest:

"Writing American history is a harmless occupation but teaching it to American schoolchildren is a political act with far-reaching consequences. The reason for this is clear. You cannot recount the past without making fundamental political judgments, and you cannot deliver those judgments without impressing them deeply on the minds of future citizens..."

With these assumptions in mind, parents should be able to discern that one of the most significant political decisions they will ever make is to decide who will teach their children history. Let us survey the historical world views that have been predominant in America at different times and analyze their significance in changing our world and our children today.

Defining the Providential View

Noah Webster, the great educator and lexicographer who compiled the first American dictionary which was released in 1828, defines Providence as: "The care and superintendence which God exercises over his creatures... Some persons admit a general providence, but deny a particular providence, not considering that a general providence consists of particulars. A belief in divine providence is a source of great consolation to good men. By divine providence is understood God himself."

As you might have surmised, Noah Webster was a devout Christian holding to the Providential view of history. Note that in his definition of Providence, Webster says that it is "a source of great consolation to good men." In this statement, he is alluding to the peace that comes from knowing that a just God presides over nations and that His plan cannot be thwarted. The opposite is also true. If you are fighting the God of history and you learn of His Providence, it can be very disconcerting!

One of the best definitions of the Providential view of history is given by the Rev. S.W. Foljambe writing in 1876. He said:

> *"It has been said that history is the biography of communities; in another and profounder sense it is the autobiography of Him 'who worketh all things after the counsel of His will' (Ephesians 1:11) and who is graciously timing all events after the counsel of His Christ, and the kingdom of God on earth."*[1]

D.W. Billington, in his book *Patterns in History*, says concerning the historical view of the Apostles, "The earliest Christians retained the attitudes to history found in the Old Testament. They continued to believe in divine intervention, to conceive of the historical process as a straight line and to see the panorama of world events as moving toward a goal."[2]

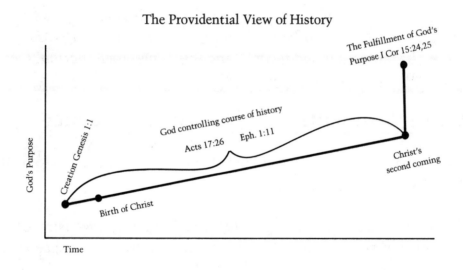

The Providential View of History

The Predominant View of Our Fathers

Our founders were surrounded by ample evidence of divine Providence and did not fail to give God the credit for both special providences and their godly institutions.

William Bradford, in his *History of Plymouth Plantation* (CHOC, p. 186) tells of the Pilgrims' reliance on Providence in the midst of their many tragedies.

> *"But these things did not dismay them (though they did sometimes trouble them) for their desires were set on the ways of God, and to enjoy His ordinances; but they rested on His Providence and knew whom they had believed."*

George Washington gave constant reference to God's Providence in his life and the life of the nation.

> *"By the miraculous care of Providence, that protected me beyond all human expectations; I had four bullets through my coat, and two horses shot under me, and yet escaped unhurt." (July 18, 1755, Writings, vol. 1, page 152).*

> *"It is the duty of all nations to acknowledge the providence of almighty God, to obey His will, to be grateful for His benefits, and humbly to implore His protection and favor." (Thanksgiving Proclamation, October 3, 1789, Writings, vol. 30, page 427).*

Our Documents Confirm His Providence

The first charter for a successful English colony was issued on April 10, 1606. The Charter of Virginia stated:

> *"We, greatly commending and graciously accepting of, the desires of the furtherance of so noble a work, which may by the Providence of almighty God, hereafter tend to the glory of His divine majesty, in propagating of Christian religion to such people, as yet live in darkness and miserable ignorance of the true knowledge and worship of God, and may in time bring the infidels and savages living in those parts, to human civility and to a settled and quiet government."*

The Fundamental Orders of Connecticut, America's first model Constitution written in 1638, begins with this statement concerning God's power and providence and then moves on to enumerate the Constitution.

"For as much as it has pleased the almighty God by the wise disposition of His divine providence so to order and dispose of things..."

The concluding statement of The Declaration of The Causes and Necessity of Taking Up Arms (Continental Congress, July 6, 1775) says:

"With a humble confidence in the mercies of the Supreme and impartial God and ruler of the universe, we most devoutly implore His divine goodness to protect us happily through this great conflict, and to dispose our adversaries to reconciliation on reasonable terms, and thereby to relieve the empire from the calamities of civil war."

The Declaration of Independence, written July 4, 1776, concludes with a similar testimony by stating:

"With a firm reliance on the protection of divine Providence."

The above examples are just a sampling of the providential view of history which held sway over much of American life well into the 19th century.

Grab-bag of Historical Theories

Most Americans, including most Christians, are products of our progressive public education system. Bored and hopeless youth drag through their civics and social studies classes deprived of the providential view under the guise of separation of church and state. The distorted views now presented in many schools are no less religious than the Providential approach; they are simply not founded on the religion of the Bible.

As a result of this educational tragedy, humanist views of history are all that we, as Americans, have been taught for generations. The humanist sees man as the decisive mover in history rather than God. These views vary greatly, and we are not suggesting that all teachers and students have imbibed them. But the religion of secular humanism has been a powerful controlling force since John Dewey and his allies gained control of the educational establishment.

In the Humanist Manifestos I and II (John Dewey was a signer of the first Manifesto), an influential group of humanists give their own definition of their theological and historical presuppositions:

"Religious humanists regard the universe as self-existing and not created...We find insufficient evidence for the belief in the existence of a supernatural; it is either meaningless or irrelevant to the question of the survival and fulfillment of the human race. As non-theists, we begin with humans, not God, nature not deity. Nature may indeed be broader and deeper than we now know; any new discoveries, however, will but enlarge our knowledge of the natural...But we can discover no divine purpose or providence for the human species. While there is much that we do not know, humans are responsible for what we are or will become. No deity will save us; we must save ourselves."[3]

Because this religious presupposition leaves its faithful devotees with no absolute standard or purpose with which to judge history, a grab-bag of historical theories vies for public acceptance.

The Cyclical View of History

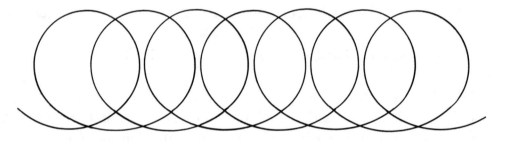

Repeating historical cycles with no ultimate purpose or goal

The Cyclical View of History

The cyclical view of history is as old as antiquity and sees the same pattern in the events of men that exists in the seasons and the life-cycle. This interpretive scheme was widely diffused in China, India, the Middle East, Greece, and Rome, and in the 1960's found its way to the American college campuses gaining wide acceptance. Its by-product, as seen in the works of such men as Nietzsche and Toynbee, are often pessimism and determinism, since all of life and culture is seen as just an endless repetition of living and dying, repeating the rhythm of the universe. Many college students, influenced by Eastern religions and historic cyclical philosophers, find themselves saying, "It doesn't matter if the bomb drops, there will be another cycle." Or, "Perhaps I'll come back as a flower." They become fatalists caught in a meaningless circle of events leading nowhere. Under the influence of this cyclical world view, the importance of individual achievement to better the world is lost in a fatalistic, all-powerful, universal cycle. Hindu societies, such as those in India, labor under this false perspective, and the people therefore have little motivation to change either the caste system or their economic poverty.

The Marxist View of History

The Marxist view of history, as defined by Marx in his *Economics and Philosophic Manuscripts of 1844*, says: *"The entire so-called history of the world is nothing but the creation of man through human labor..."* His anti-Christian interpretive scheme and that of his protegés has subtly permeated not only the communist world but American culture. This historical materialism sees man as an economic unit caught in a class struggle.

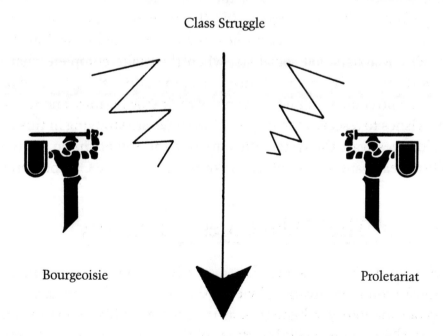

Class Struggle

Bourgeoisie   Proletariat

Resulting in the "Perfect Socialist State"

One follower of Marx, Charles Beard (one of the most prolific materialist historians), molded the Hegelian dialectic and Marxist theory into scores of his historical works on American history. He de-emphasized the Christian influence upon our founding, while debunking the character of our founders. The main thread that he saw in American history was illustrated in the title of his first major work, *An Economic Interpretation of the Constitution*.

Most of the readers of this book, whether they know it or not, have been deeply influenced by this view of history. Docu-dramas such as "Roots," "The Rebels," "The Bastard" and many other dramas on the television screen also portray history as a race conflict or class struggle between rich and poor. There is no doubt that most of these programs, watched by hundreds of millions of Americans, reflect the influence of men such as Beard and the Marxist view of history. Their influence cannot be under-estimated. *U.S. News and World Report*, May 21, 1979, tells us that most Americans believe any docu-dramas they see on the television screen. Is it any wonder that many of our people are down on America and its free enterprise system and see little hope for the future? The Marxist historian or writer is taught to be adept at exaggerating the evils of free enterprise (robber barons, etc.) and denying the fundamental base of our society: Biblical principles and their influence on and through individuals.

At this point it is important to indicate that all historical views which deny the sovereignty of the God of the Bible must of necessity distort the facts of history to fit their perspective. They become revisionists and will often tolerate many views, except one – the Providential view. This helps to explain why Marxists and socialists, when they take complete charge of a nation will often purge many of the people, including the educated and the Christians who could remind the people of their true heritage and roots. If the student wishes to research the impact of what we are studying in this chapter, he should investigate the systematic purges in the Soviet Union (between 30-50 million dead), and the annihilation of millions of the Cambodian people in 1975.

The "Who Cares" Mentality

Other humanist views include: progressive history, historicism, and one of the most prominent historical views, the existential, "who cares" historical-drop-out mentality. If history is, as the renowned historian, Edward Gibbons, said, the recounting of the crimes of the human species, why study it? Today millions of Americans dislike history because they see it as irrelevant. "Today is what counts" and "We learn from history that we learn nothing from history" are typical cliches tossed around by bored history students who see their lives as autonomous units or chance evolutionary happenings.

The Existential View of History

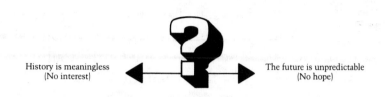

History is meaningless
(No interest)

The future is unpredictable
(No hope)

Existential Moment
"eat, drink, and be merry for tomorrow we die."

Many Christians Are Caught

Many Christians have subconsciously adopted the existential view of history (as graphed above). They de-emphasize their importance in a God-ordained historical chain of Christianity and see themselves simply as individuals God has plucked out of an evil world who are now just awaiting heaven. Their sense of responsibility for the past and their hope and planning for the building of the future are lost in the "now generation" where they are called to focus on self-improvement. This attitude covers the burden of guilt that lays heavily on the head of American Christians, but it does not alleviate their responsibility for our nation's crisis. The more deeply we pursue this study, the more it will become evident that it is not the humanists, Communists, or social deviates who are responsible for our present condition. Because these people are lost, we should not be surprised if they act like lost and bitter rebels. But it is the Christian community that has neglected its heritage and forgotten the history – God's history – of America. We are the ones who should be expected to remember it and restore a knowledge of it to the American people as a whole. Until the Christian comes to grips with his historical duties, denouncing his existential perspective and reaffirming the providential view of history, the renewal of our nation will be impossible.

Let us survey a few of the "Gilgal stones" (Josh. 4:19-24) and "landmarks of our fathers" (Prov. 22:28, 23:10) that defy the humanists' explanation and can help to rebuild our faith and the faith of our children in the great God of Providence.

Providential Landing at Cape Cod

The landing of the Pilgrims at Cape Cod was an important providential event, for they were bound for Virginia! But the Mayflower was blown hundreds of miles off its course and ended up instead at Cape Cod. Because their patent did not include this territory, they consulted with the Captain of the Mayflower and "resolved to stand for the southward...to find some place about Hudson's River for their habitation." But God did not allow them to do so. They soon encountered "dangerous shoals and roaring breakers" and were forced to return to Cape Cod. From there they began their scouting expeditions to find a place to settle and finally discovered what is now Plymouth. Had they arrived a few years earlier they would have been greeted by the fiercest tribe in the region, but in 1617 the Patuxet tribe which had occupied the area had been wiped out by a plague. It was perhaps the only place where they could have survived.[4]

"A Special Instrument Sent of God"

This leads to another major providential event in the lives of the Pilgrims. There was *one* survivor of the Patuxet tribe, and how he survived shows the Hand of God in history. This Indian, named Squanto, was kidnapped in 1605 by Captain Weymouth and taken to England. Here he learned English and in 1614 he returned to New England on an expedition with Captain John Smith. Though Smith wanted to return him to his people, this was not God's timing. Shortly after Smith left for England, Squanto was again kidnapped.[5] Captain Thomas Hunt lured Squanto and 24 other Indians on board his ship and, according to Bradford, intended to sell them into slavery in Spain. "But he [Squanto] got away for England and was entertained by a merchant in London, and employed to Newfoundland and other parts, and lastly brought hither into these parts by [Captain] Dermer."[6] Dermer was on a voyage of discovery on the New England coast in 1618 and probably intended to use him as an interpreter with the Indians, but Squanto apparently jumped ship and headed for Plymouth – only to find that all of his tribe had been wiped out by the plague. After searching in vain for survivors, he attached himself to the neighboring tribe of the Wampanoag. Fluent in English, he was led of God to offer his friendship and help to the Pilgrims when he learned of their presence at Plymouth. He joined with them thereafter and was converted to Christianity. Bradford says that he "was a special instrument sent of God for their good beyond their expectation."[7] Without Squanto's help they might not have survived for he showed them how to plant corn, fertilizing it with fish. He also acted as their guide and, most important, was their interpreter in their dealings with the Wampanoag chief, Massasoit, in the crucial early days when it was vitally important to the Pilgrims to establish friendly relations with their Indian neighbors. With Squanto's aid as interpreter, a peace treaty that lasted 50 years was agreed upon, which treated both Indians and Pilgrims justly under the law. Through the hand of God, the Pilgrims did not share the fate of other English colonies in the New World which were wiped out by hostile Indians. (See CHOC, pp. 206-7)

"New England Stood Still and Saw the Salvation of God"

Moving to a later period of America's history, during the colonizing attempts of France, we encounter another striking instance of God's providence. Wherever the French went, they allowed only the Roman Catholic religion to be practiced, and the New Englanders greatly feared them. The Stuart monarchs in England were sympathetic to France's Catholic monarch, but when a firmly protestant king, William of Orange, ascended the English throne, the French began to attack the English colonists in America with great savagery. The New England forces, with the aid of a British squadron, captured Louisbourg in Nova Scotia. Here God used the weather to the advantage of the New Englanders. "The English Appear to have enlisted Heaven in their interest," wrote one of the town's residents later. "So long as the expedition lasted they had the most beautiful weather in the world." No storms, no unfavorable winds, and – no fog which was most surprising for the area. After the capture of Louisbourg, the French sent half of their navy under the command of the Duc d'Anville "to lay waste the whole seacoast from Nova Scotia to Georgia."[8]

The Rev. Thomas Prince, pastor of the South Church in Boston later preached a sermon of Thanksgiving for God's protecting hand when New England was "a long while wholly ignorant of their designs against us..."[9] Even when rumors reached them, they were not greatly worried because they understood that the British fleet would prevent the French from leaving the shores of France. But, unknown to the colonists, the French eluded Admiral

Martin's squadron and slipped out to sea. But, as Rev. Prince observed: "While we knew nothing of Danger, God beheld it, and was working Salvation for us. And when we had none to help in *America,* He even prevented our Friends in *Europe* from coming to succour us; that we might see our Salvation was *his* Work alone, and that the Glory belongs entirely to Him."[10]

Having eluded the British, the proud French fleet "of about 70 sail" put to sea on June 20, 1746. As the vessels crossed the Atlantic, heading for Halifax, they were delayed at first in a prolonged calm and then encountered storms in which several ships were disabled by lightning. Pestilence broke out; then the entire fleet was scattered to the four winds by tremendous storms. By this means, "they were...so dispersed in the midst of the Ocean that by Aug. 26, they had left but twelve Ships of the Line and forty-one others...."[11] On Sept. 2, as they were nearing the dangerous shoals off the Isle of Sables, they encountered another violent storm and lost several more vessels.

When the Duc d'Anville's ship finally reached Halifax (or Chebucto, as it was then called), a lonely, isolated area, he fully expected to rendezvous with other French ships sent from the West Indies to meet him. The West Indies Squadron had indeed been there, but discouraged by the long delay of d'Anville's fleet, had given up and left!

During all this, what had the New England colonists been doing? Another New England pastor, Rev. Jonathan French, writes that as soon as the French vessels were sighted off the coast, the people were "filled with consernation. The streets filled with men, marching for the defence of the sea ports, and the distresses of women and children, trembling for the event, made...deep impressions upon the minds of those who remember these scenes. But never did the religion, for which the country was settled, appear more important, nor prayer more prevalent, than on this occasion. A prayer-hearing God, stretched forth the arm of His power, and destroyed that mighty Armament, in a manner almost as extraordinary as the drowning of Pharoah and his host in the Red Sea."[12]

What happened was this: Shortly after his arrival at Halifax, the Duc d'Anville was so appalled at the loss of the major part of his fleet "and finding his few Ships so shattered, so many Men dead, so many sickly, and no more of his Fleet come in; he sunk into discouragement, and Sept. 15 died; but in such a Condition...it was generally tho't he poysoned himself, and was buried without Ceremony."[13] More ships finally limped into port, but many of the men on board were ill and their food supplies were fast running out. The commander who took d'Anville's place committed suicide only days after their arrival by falling on his own sword. The third in command ordered the men ashore to recruit French and Indians so that an attack on Annapolis could proceed. But before they could leave Halifax, 2,000 or 3,000 men died of a pestilence. Finally, the fleet's new commander, La Jonquiere, set sail on October 13, 1746 intending to attack Annapolis. He was probably unaware of the fact that on October 6, the New England colonies had set October 16 as a day of Fasting and Prayer for their deliverance.

Rev. French describes the events that followed: "On this great emergency, and day of darkness and doubtful expectation, the 16th of October was observed as a day of FASTING AND PRAYER throughout the Province. And, wonderful to relate, that very night God sent upon them a more dreadful storm than either of the former, and completed their destruction. Some overset, some foundered, and a remnant only of this miserable fleet returned to France to carry the news. Thus NEW ENGLAND STOOD STILL, AND SAW THE SALVATION OF GOD."[14] (See Ex. 14:13)

The Hand of God Rescues George Washington's Army

God's providence played a great part in rescuing General Washington's troops when they were penned up in Brooklyn Heights by General Howe in the early days of the Revolution. Despite the heavy losses General Howe had inflicted on Washington's army, he had not succeeded in capturing or destroying it. Now he prepared to lay siege to the American forces on Long Island: some 8,000 men on Brooklyn Heights. Washington realized he must retreat. But how? The English forces surrounded him in a great semi-circle and behind him British ships could close him off at any time. Then began Washington's desperate, bold strategy. He collected every vessel he could find from row boats to sloops and, manned by fishermen from Gloucester and Marblehead, he set about to evacuate his troops by night. A desperate measure, surely, and one doomed to failure. For would not the British see them in the moonlight or hear the splashing of their oars and the many sounds of 8,000 men being transported, however quiet they tried to be!? But, as historian John Fiske writes: "The Americans had been remarkably favored by the sudden rise of a fog which covered the East River..."[15]

In the morning, the British discovered to their astonishment that their enemies had vanished – even taking with them their provisions, horses, and cannons! Fiske maintains that "So rare a chance of ending the war at a blow was never again to be offered to the British commanders." But, at the crucial, desperate moment, when Washington had done all he could do, the Hand of God intervened, providing the critically-needed elements so that neither by *sight* nor by *sound* were the army's whereabouts known to the enemy.

Were all these events "happy accidents" or mere "good luck"? When these and hundreds more striking instances of the providential hand of God in our history are put side by side, a pattern emerges that shows God's repeated protection of the new nation whose settlers had founded it for His glory.

"With a Firm Reliance on Divine Providence"

The Founding Fathers were keenly aware of God's providence and took care to see that the Declaration of Independence ended with this phrase: "And for the support of this Declaration, with a firm reliance on the Protection of Divine Providence, we mutually pledge to each other our Lives, our Fortunes and our Sacred Honor."

During the Constitutional Convention, not only did Benjamin Franklin appeal for daily prayers that they might be worthy of the support of Divine Providence, but George Washington, too, interrupted arguments favoring half-way methods to patch up the poorly-working Confederation rather than to follow through with a real plan of union. He rose from his presidential chair to his full, imposing height and, his voice trembling with emotion, he declared: "If to please the people, we offer what we ourselves disapprove, how can we afterward defend our work? Let us raise a standard to which the wise and the honest can repair; the event is in the hand of God!"

His words were a bracing reminder of the need for high resolve if they were to be worthy of God's providential support. "From that moment," says historian John Fiske, "the mood in which they worked caught something from the glorious spirit of Washington."[16]

In conclusion, let us encourage you to continue to read and study the untold story of America's Christian history from the original documents, many of which are included in CHOC and T&L. There you will find many other events that demonstrate our Founding Fathers' "firm reliance upon Divine Providence." It should be noted that because of their historical perspective and reliance upon God, the hope of reformation and victory was always before the early settlers of America.

Today as we once again recount the mighty deeds of God on our behalf and give Him the glory for these deeds, we too can expect a wave of hope to sweep our nation. The God of Abraham, Isaac and Jacob who preserved our forefathers as they covenanted to establish a nation for His honor, can, if He wills, turn hostile missiles back into silos and renew the hearts of a repentant people in the critical decade of the 1980's.

Notes:

1. Verna M. Hall, comp., *Christian History of The American Revolution: Consider and Ponder* (San Francisco: Foundation for American Christian Education, 1976), p. 47.
2. D.W. Billington, *Patterns in History* (Donners Grove, Illinois: Inter-Varsity Press, 1979), p. 48.
3. *Humanist Manifestos I and II* (Buffalo, New York: Prometheus Books, 1977).
4. William Bradford, *Of Plymouth Plantation*, ed. Samuel Eliot Morison (New York: The Modern Library, 1967), Chapter XI.
5. Bradford Smith, *Bradford of Plymouth* (Philadelphia and New York: J. B. Lippincott Co., 1951, p. 189.
6. Bradford, *Of Plymouth Planatation*, p. 81.
7. Ibid.
8. George M. Wrong, *The Conquest of New France* (New Haven: University Press, 1918), pp. 82-91
9. *Mr. Prince's Thanksgiving Sermon on the Salvation of God in 1746* (Boston: D. Henchman, 1746), p. 21.
10. Ibid., p. 27.
11. Ibid., p. 28.
12. Rev. Jonathan French, *Thanksgiving Sermon, November 29, 1798*, quoted in Hall, *Christian History of the American Revolution*, p. 51.
13. Prince, p. 29.
14. Hall, *Christian History of the American Revolution*, p. 51.
15. John Fiske, *The American Revolution*, 2 vols. (Boston and New York: Houghton, Mifflin & Co., 1898), I:212.
16. John Fiske, *The Critical Period of American History: 1783-1789* (Boston and New York: Houghton, Mifflin & Co., 1898), pp. 231-32.

Further Reading – Chapter 2

Chapter 2 – Study Questions:

1. Can you paraphrase the Providential view of history in terms that explain its personal application and influence upon you as an individual? _____

   _____

   _____

2. The authors have admitted to a distinctive Christian historical perspective claiming that neutrality is impossible. Is this statement, applied to historical study, also true of all areas of life? Why are Biblical presuppositions necessary to study man, English, economics, etc.? _____

   _____

   _____

3. Compare Noah Webster's definition of "providence" in his 1828 dictionary with definitions given by later editions after his death. What is the impact of the definition of words? See, for example, comparative definitions of "sovereignty" and "love." _____

   _____

   _____

4. What lifestyles are encouraged by the various historical world views? Which world view do you hold to and which is most prevalent in your circles? _____

   _____

   _____

5. Why can the Christian better comprehend such providential events as those mentioned in this chapter? And, why are these events left out of all major histories that students read today? _____

   _____

   _____

Chapter 3

America is Not the End of the World

"Lastly, (and which was not least,) a great hope & inward zeall they had of laying some good foundation, or at least to make some way thereunto, for ye propagating & advancing ye gospell of ye kingdom of Christ in those remote parts of ye world; yea, though they should be but even as stepping-stones unto others for ye performing of so great a work"

Gov. William Bradford,
History of Plymouth Plantation

45

JOHN WYCLIFFE, THE MORNING STAR OF THE REFORMATION

"The real Reformation began 150 years before Martin Luther hammered his famous theses onto the Church door at Wittenberg. It began in England with John Wycliffe who is rightly called 'the morning star of the Reformation.'...He began to see that his efforts to reform the Church were doomed to failure, for only as the people had the Word of God could they begin to reform their own lives and then, as the next logical step, the life of the Church...Now, without waiting to gather a committee of scholars to tackle the immense task Wycliffe began alone to translate the Bible into English finishing his translation in 1381....Through Wycliffe's Bible, an entire nation was awakened out of religious torpor and given a new sense of purpose."

Chapter 3

America is Not
the End of the World

It has been mentioned in previous chapters that the American people have forgotten the "ancient landmarks" of their fathers (Prov. 22:28). Now, however, there are many Americans again remembering the God of the Bible and what He did in the founding of their nation. The study you are engaged in is part of this renewing process. But before we proceed into the specific history of our nation we should discuss two foundational truths that will help provide a broad perspective on the study of history: the purpose of God in history and the Chain of Christianity.

God's Purpose in History

What is God's purpose in history? Those who do not share the Providential approach to history spoken of in the last chapter would say that there is no definitive purpose to history. They would see autonomous man making history or some fatalistic impersonal force. God's overall plan for His world, man, and all His creation – which is being accomplished in history – is seen in passages such as I Peter 4:11: "If any man speak, let him speak as the oracle of God: if any man minister, let him do it as of the ability that God giveth; that God in all things may be glorified through Jesus Christ, to whom be praise and dominion for ever."

Our job then, as stewards, fulfilling God's will in history, is to do all things to the glory of God (I Cor. 10:31). The Westminster Catechism beautifully summarizes our purpose in light of God's plan which is to "glorify God and to enjoy Him forever."

His Will – Our Commission

Our Great Commission is clearly given in Matt. 28:18-20 where we are told to make disciples of all nations, teaching them to observe all things that Christ has commanded. Our job then is not evangelism alone (as important as this primary task is), but to see that through the Gospel, nations as well as individuals rise up and glorify God and obey His Son.

Matthew Henry, the great Bible commentator read by our founders, said concerning this passage in Matthew: "What is the principal intention of this commission; to *disciple* all nations. 'Admit them disciples; do your utmost to make the nations Christian nations.'...The work which the apostles had to do, was, to set up the Christian religion in all places, and it was honourable work; the achievements of the mighty heroes of the world were nothing to it. They conquered the nations for themselves, and made them miserable; the apostles conquered them for Christ, and made them happy."[1]

Governor Bradford shared this perspective saying that the Pilgrims saw themselves as "stepping-stones" for God's purpose. That is a Great Commission and one that has provided the primary impetus to Christian civilization as the "Chain of Christianity" has moved around the world.

As we begin to examine specific links in this chain as it moved Westward, it is important to remember that the spread of Christian culture is predicated upon one major driving force: that God may be glorified through the preaching of the Gospel (Matt. 28:18-20) and the subduing of His world (Gen. 1:26-28). Of course, there have also been carnal motives for cultural development that have influenced western culture, i.e. greed, lust, survival, curiosity, but none as powerful, consistent, or driving as God's commission.

The Chain of Christianity

The Chain of Christianity is the observed phenomena of the spreading of the Gospel of Christ as it took root historically. In this chapter we are going to focus upon God's preparation of the continents, His preparation of His people, and the groundwork He laid for the building of a nation.

But first let us survey the historical movement of Christianity. The story begins with the primitive church spreading the Gospel of Christ to all of the known world before 70 A.D. (see Rom 1:8 and Col. 1:6,23). It should be noted that although the Gospel was preached to the four corners of the earth, it only became the dominant cultural influence to the west of Jerusalem. The Apostle Paul in Acts 16:9 documents the first westward movement of the Gospel when God directed him to the West in a vision where a man from Macedonia appealed to him saying: "Come over to Macedonia and help us."

John Quade gives us a survey of the progress of the chain from the time of Paul.

"The Chain of Christianity crossed the Mediterranean, moved into Northern Europe, and westward through the Gauls, leaped into the English Channel and there it paused until the next link in the chain was about to be formed. The Gospel then leaped the Atlantic and formed the basis of a new form of government entirely unique in the history of man. It crossed America in the 19th century and until recently paused before crossing the Pacific to Japan, Korea, and Southeast Asia."[2]

Charles Bancroft, an historian from the last century, saw this westward course, writing in 1879:

"We see here again the operation of that constant law that impelled men, or moved the 'Star of Empire,' westward. The form of the continents, the character of the surface and the climate, provided a natural and desirable opening only in that direction. The overplus of population, the discontent of some part of the people with existing government, the restlessness of adventurers, or the requirements of trade and commerce produced a migration." (CHOC, pp. 6-7)

If you have a copy of Christian History of the Constitution (CHOC), turn to page 6A and observe the diagram of the Chain of Christianity. Read the "landmarks" of its progress. Note that the chain has not been fully extended to Asia. The great Dutch theologian and statesman, Abraham Kuyper, lecturing at Princeton in 1898, gave the reason for the impeded progress of the chain. "Its westward course through China and Japan is impeded...by modernism [weak Christianity]." He was referring to the fact that the liberating truth of Christianity had not crossed the Pacific due to the failure of American Christianity to recover its purpose.

America a Link – Not the Kingdom

When all of history is seen as the unveiling of God's purpose within time and space, America's Christian history and the liberty that it produced can be viewed in a much more strategic light. Seen in the context of God's greater plan for the whole world, America can be placed in its proper perspective as a link on the chain, a vessel for God's use, but not the pinnacle of history. America is not the final expression of the kingdom of God, but it has been the highest expression of Christian culture the world has known to date which makes its study extremely important.

No Racism or Manifest Destiny

It is not our intention to portray Americans as God's chosen people or nation, as some modern religious cults have suggested. Nor are we trying to suggest America has a "manifest destiny" or that she is destined to rule because of some inherent greatness. The idea of a "manifest destiny" grew up in the 19th century as a secularization of the original Pilgrim covenant and Puritan hope. God's purpose for America can be clearly seen in history through the covenants of our people and divine intervention in events.

That purpose is molded by the hand of the Creator and it is to His glory if we as a nation have been used to spread his Gospel. Our forefathers understood that our commission was to spread the message of Christ to the world and build a Biblically-based civilization; they also understood that if they denied their commission, God would surely judge them and their culture. America's current condition is evidence of that judgment.

God Prepares the Continents

We must go back to the beginning to see the full context of God's plan and, specifically, how America fits into that plan. We must go back to the first book of the Bible. Is America included there? Yes, in the very first verse: "In the beginning God created the heavens and the earth." This land mass now called North America has been here from the time of the creation, separated from the other continents, by two vast oceans. But did God create the continents for His purposes?

In Job 38, God, speaking to Job says: "Where were you when I laid the foundations of the earth. Tell me, if you have understanding. Who set its measurements, since you know?" Our God not only laid out the dimensions of the world, setting the boundaries of the sea (Job 38:10), but He has determined the appointed times and places of every nation and people. Acts 17:26 says, "He made from one, every nation of mankind to live on all the face of the earth, having determined their appointed times, and the boundaries of their habitations."

Christian historians and scientists of the last century clearly saw the Hand of God in the creation and preservation not only of His world in general, but specifically of the North American continent. Arnold Guyot, eminent geographer from Harvard, wrote in 1873:

> "But, gentlemen, it is not enough to have seized, in this point of view, entirely physical as yet, the functions of the great masses of the continents. They have others, still more important, which, if rightly understood, ought to be considered as the final end for which they have received their existence. To understand and appreciate them at their full value, to study them in their true point of view, we must rise to a higher position. We must elevate ourselves to the moral world to understand the physical world: the physical world has no meaning except by and for the moral world..." (T&L, p. 142)

After analyzing the climates, natural resources, division of the oceans, the configuration of the rivers and mountains in light of God's Gospel purpose and the westward movement of Christianity, Guyot concludes concerning America:

> "America, different in position, structure, and climatic conditions, from both the other northern continents, seems destined to play a part in the history of mankind unlike that of Europe and Asia, though not less noble than either...America, therefore, with her cultured and progressive people, and her social organization, founded upon the principle of the equality and brotherhood of all mankind, seems destined to furnish the most complete expression of the Christian civilization..." (CHOC, p. 4)

Great historians of our history also saw the obvious Hand of God in the forming of this continent in such a way that it would be preserved for a unique, Biblically-minded and Christian people.

Emma Willard, historian, educator, and early pioneer for women's rights to higher education (see CHOC page 438) writes in her *History of the United States*: "In observing the United States, there is much to convince us, that an Almighty over-ruling Providence, designed from the first, to place here a great, united people." (T&L, p. 153)

After a trip here in the 1830's, Alexis De Tocqueville wrote concerning this continent in his book *American Institutions and Their Influence*:

> "Although the vast country which we have been describing was inhabited by many indigenous tribes, it may justly be said, at the time of its

51

discovery by Europeans, to have formed one great desert. The Indians occupied, without possessing it...Those coasts so admirably adapted for commerce and industry; those wide and deep rivers; that inexhaustible valley of the Mississippi; the whole continent, in short, seemed prepared to be the abode of a great nation, yet unborn." (T&L, p. 153).

At this point the reader may be asking the question "did God prepare only the American continent?" The obvious answer is no. He prepared all the continents for His greater plan (see T&L page 142-153 and CHOC pages 3-39).

God Prepares a People

After observing the way God has set the stage of history through geography and climate, we must trace the movement of the Chain of Christianity through God's most powerful and eternal creation. The center stage of world history, when seen from a Christian perspective, is not dominated by class struggles, race wars, or the whim of potentates, but is flooded with light and meaning from the lives of simple believers in the Most High God. These self-governing Christians have been and continue to be today, the most powerful world-changing force known to man.

We will be observing these men and women throughout our study as God prepares them to fulfill His purpose. In this chapter we focus upon how this self-governing Christian was prepared to expand God's kingdom as the Word of God was put into his hands.

The New Testament Church

Most histories of antiquity give but a few lines to the impact of the people of this new religion, "Christianity," inaugurated in 30 A.D. by Jesus Christ. The failure to recognize the historic centrality of the New Testament churches is evidence that man looks on the outside but God looks upon the heart (I Sam. 16:7).

First, God set his people free from the bondage of sin and guilt which had kept them as slaves (John 8:32-36). This internal liberty, accomplished through faith in Christ's atoning death and victorious ascension, made men free, whether in a Philippian jail (Acts 16:25) or in a stone quarry awaiting execution (Act 7:54). This internal liberty, however, was finally to have its external manifestation on a national scale and it was the Word of God unleashed in the hands of the individual that would, in time, liberate every area of life both internal and external. Jesus Christ announced His plan to liberate men internally and externally in the first sermon of His ministry where He said:

"The spirit of the Lord is upon me, because He has anointed me to preach the Gospel to the poor; He has sent me to heal the broken-hearted, and to preach deliverance to the captives, and the recovery of sight to the blind, to set at liberty them that are bruised." (Luke 4:18)

The New Testament Churches – Little Republics

Through the teachings of Jesus Christ, the inspired Gospels and Epistles, and a renewed commitment to God's Law (the Old Testament) the primitive churches were able to break with the Pagan view of man which dominated the world. They demonstrated the Christian view of man in their churches which became "little Christian Republics." Leonard Bacon says in his book *The Genesis of the New England Churches*, "There are indications that in every place the society of believers in Christ was a little republic." (CHOC, p. 16) Women, slaves, gentiles, and children were all seen as important in the decisions of the church; even the choice of leadership was the responsibility of the people, not an episcopacy or a national church. (Read CHOC pages 16-28).

These primitive believers began to "turn the world upside down" (Acts 17:6). It took time. They didn't have a completed Bible and most could not read; they were under cruel persecution for almost 300 years, and they had no recent examples to follow. They were like the mustard seed that Jesus spoke of as the smallest in the field but that would one day grow up into a tree where the birds of the air would lodge. The Kingdom of God was growing and nothing could stop it. (Matt. 13:31)

Dominion Without the Word

The Word of God which had been completed by the Apostles in the first century was officially canonized in the third and fourth centuries. Having a completed Word, great church philosophers, such as Augustine, were able to perceive a Christian world view that rocked pagan culture with its cyclical view of history and gave Christianity a strong impetus.

The so-called Dark Ages saw a continued spread of the Chain of Christianity. Paganism in Europe and England was overthrown and Christian civilization became predominant. Even though the Word of God was not in the hands of the common man, it was preserved in monasteries. The stage was being set for a full-scale reformation, as for the first time in history, the Bible would be united with the individual on a national scale.

The Morning Star of the Reformation

The real Reformation began 150 years before Martin Luther hammered his famous Theses onto the Church door at Wittenberg. It began in England with John Wycliffe who is rightly called "the morning star of the Reformation." (See CHOC, p. 28B) Wycliffe was educated at Oxford University where he became a professor of divinity. He first gained prominence by his efforts to reform the Church in England which had become corrupt and riddled with superstition. He was persecuted for his attempts but was saved from death through his friendship with a powerful nobleman.

The First Bible in English

Expelled from Oxford, he retired to a country pastorate. He began to see that his efforts at external reform of the Church were doomed to failure, for only as the people had the Word of God could they begin to reform their own lives and then, as the next logical step, the life of the church. But the Bible could only be read by the educated clergy and nobility because it was only available in Latin. Now, without waiting to gather a committee of scholars to tackle the immense task, Wycliffe began alone to translate the Bible into English, finishing his translation in 1381.

Taking the Bible to the People

As he translated the Scriptures, he pondered the pressing problem of how to get God's Word to the people despite the opposition of court and clergy. He was led of God to found a religious order of Poor Preachers who took his tracts and portions of the Bible, as he translated it, and distributed them to the people throughout England. The people flocked to meetings on village greens, in chapels, and halls, where the preachers read aloud to them from the Bible. But now the preachers were confronted by another serious hurdle: few of the common people could read.

Literacy Program of the Poor Preachers

Undeterred, the preachers set about to teach the people to read, instructing men, women, and children, so that they could understand the Scriptures for themselves. One observer who disapproved of God's Word being put into the hands of the common people wrote indignantly that Wycliffe's Bible had "become more accessible and familiar to laymen and to women able to read than it had...been to the most intelligent and learned of the clergy..." (T&L, p. 166)

Such opponents called his Poor Preachers and their followers "Lollards," a scornful name meaning "idle babblers." But Lollardy penetrated deeply into English life, so much so that soon followers of Wycliffe were everywhere and among all classes of people from poor farmers and artisans to noblemen. One panic-stricken opponent claimed: "Every second man one meets is a Lollard!"[3]

An Entire Nation Awakened

Through Wycliffe's Bible, an entire nation was awakened out of religious torpor and given a new sense of purpose. But, at last, the Pope summoned Wycliffe to Rome to undergo trial before the Papal Court. He was too old and ill to go, however, and died December 31, 1384 while ministering to his parish church. But Lollardy continued long after his death as a sort of underground movement emerging into full light again in the time of the Pilgrims and Puritans.

The hatred of his enemies followed Wycliffe beyond the grave. In 1425, 41 years after his death, the church ordered his bones exhumed and burned, together with some 200 books he had written. His ashes were cast into the River Swift which flows near Lutterworth and "the little river conveyed Wycliffe's remains into the Avon, the Avon into the Severn, Severn into the narrow seas, they to the main oceans. And thus the ashes of Wycliffe are the emblem of his doctrine, which now is dispersed all the world over." (T&L, p. 168)

In the next 200 years, many of God's finest would give their lives for the furtherance of God's purpose, not seeing the full fruition of Christian liberty, but heralding its coming.

The Plowman and the Pope

Although faced with intense opposition, William Tyndale, a scholar educated at both Oxford and Cambridge, persisted in his plan to translate the Scriptures into the English of his time which had changed greatly since Wycliffe's day.

55

"One man, desirous of reviving the Church of Christ in England, had made the translation of the Holy Scriptures the work of his life. Tyndale had been forced to leave his country; but he had left it only to prepare seed which, borne on the wings of the wind, was to change the wilderness of Great Britain into a fruitful garden." (T&L, p. 334)

In 1525, his translation of the New Testament from the original Greek, rather than the Latin version used by Wycliffe, was published in Germany. Then he began work on the Old Testament.

"He felt pressed to accomplish a vow made many years before. 'If God preserves my life,' he had said, 'I will cause a boy that driveth a plow to know more of the Scriptures than the pope.'" (T&L, p. 334)

October 6, 1536, Vilvorde, Belgium: After many years of toil, William Tyndale's translation of the Word of God in the language of the English people was nearly completed. Before it could be published or distributed, Tyndale was burned at the stake as a religious heretic at the behest of King Henry VIII of England. As the fire raged, Tyndale preached a sermon calling to his King to believe in Christ. "Lord, open the King of England's eyes!" were his last words. (See T&L, p. 336)

Within twelve months of Tyndale's death, this same King Henry, having broken with the Roman church, was advised that he needed his own Bible in every parish in the land to prove his independence from the Pope. Tyndale's version was submitted to the king. Then, as Reformation historian D'Aubigne relates, something remarkable happened:

"Henry ran over the book: Tyndale's name was not in it, and the dedication to his Majesty was very well written. The King regarding...Holy Scripture as the most powerful engine to destroy the papal system...came to an unexpected resolution: he authorized the sale and the reading of the Bible throughout the kingdom..." (T&L, p. 336)

Henry little dreamed that he had just laid a time-bomb under his own tyrannical throne by giving the Word of God to the people! Tyndale had won the victory. Once again God had taken the wrath of men to praise him. (Ps. 76:10)

56

Extending the Chain

At the same time on the continent the great reformers, Luther, Calvin, Zwingli, and others began to give a systematic explanation of God's purpose for man and the way of salvation through faith alone. (Read T&L page 166-172). Their intelligent, Bible-centered faith was captured 100 years later by the Pilgrims and Puritans in England.

At the proper time, a small band of these Scripturists was chosen by God to forge the next link in God's movement of the Gospel. The Pilgrims came here in 1620, but thousands of years of godly wisdom had preceded them. The discoveries of Columbus and inventions such as the sea compass made their travels possible. The invention of the printing press by Gutenberg, the printing of the Geneva and King James Bibles made it possible for each family to have a Bible of their own, setting the stage for the self-government of the future.

It was an insignificant band of English farmers and artisans who set foot on Plymouth on December 12, 1620, but they had within their character all the elements necessary to lay the foundation of the world's first Christian Constitutional Republic.

In the following chapters specific principles, people, and events that produced this nation will be explored, but let us close this chapter with a vision of the future development of the Chain of Christianity.

Forging the Next Link

We mentioned earlier that America is but one link in God's Chain of Christianity. To the extent that we Americans, have forgotten our history, and therefore God's purpose for our nation, to that degree we have lost God's blessing upon our land. America was blessed because our fathers covenanted before God to fulfill His Gospel purpose.

If we are to save our nation, it will take more than personal repentance and revival, as important as this first step is (II Chron. 7:14). We also will need to re-discover our place in the historic Chain of Christianity and to help forge the next link. John Quade gives this thought-provoking perspective on the potential future as God's truth moves westward.

"Even 10 years ago, it would have been a preposterous thought for any Christian to consider that in 1981 the largest Christian church in the history of man would be found in Seoul, South Korea, but nevertheless,

there it sits, with more than 33% of the nation now classified as Christians. Right in the middle of the empire of Buddhism and just a few hundred miles from mainland Red China. Is there any doubt in any readers' mind that the next link to the Chain of Christianity has already been cast and is even now being broken from its mold?"[4]

Notes:

1. Matthew Henry, Commentary on the Whole Bible, VI vols. (Old Tappan, New Jersey: Fleming Revell Co.), 5:446.
2. John Quade, *UP Magazine* (Spring 1981).
3. J.R. Green, *Short History of the English People*, New York and London: Harper & Bros., 1898), p. 242.
4. John Quade, *UP Magazine* (Spring 1981).

Further Reading – Chapter 3

Chapter 3 – Study Questions

1. What is God's purpose in history? _____

   _____

   _____

2. What is your responsibility in helping to fulfill that purpose? _____

   _____

   _____

3. Is the Great Commission applicable to nations as well as individuals? _

   _____

   _____

4. Is America the "last act" in the geographic development of Christianity?

_____

_____

5. What progressive purposes of God can you discover in His development of the different continents? _____

_____

_____

6. Were early American Christians aware of the Hand of God in the forming of our continent? _____

_____

_____

7. During the Reformation what was the major tool God gave to the individual to help him transform his life and his society? _____

_____

_____

8. What was the governmental form of the early Christian church? _____

_____

_____

9. How many inventions and Providential events can you think of that have moved the Chain of Christianity to its present position? _____

_____

_____

10. What effect did the translation of the Bible by Wycliffe and Tyndale have on the individual? _____

_____

_____

11. What current events indicate a movement toward completing the Chain of Christianity? _____

_____

_____

Chapter 4

The Individual Set Free

"If ye continue in my word, then are ye my disciples indeed; And ye shall know the truth, and the truth shall make you free."

John 8:32

THE PILGRIMS AT PRAYER

"They shook off this yoke of antichristian bondage, and as the Lord's free people, joined themselves by a covenant of the Lord into a church estate in the fellowship of the gospel, to walk in all His ways, made known or to be made known unto them, according to their best endeavours, whatsoever it should cost them, the Lord assisting them."

– William Bradford
Of Plymouth Plantation

Chapter 4

The Individual
Set Free

For several decades most of us in America have been sheltered from facing the life or death decision faced by many of our forefathers: "Give me liberty or give me death!"

Today, most of us take for granted such things as our individual liberty: the right to make what we wish of our life; to choose a profession; to live and work where we wish; to pursue happiness in our own way and enjoy the fruits of our labors; to own our own homes and put money into savings accounts or investments in businesses that provide goods or services of benefit to everyone; and above all, the right to worship God according to the dictates of our conscience. But we have forgotten that liberty was not always alive and well in the world. In fact, liberty is a relatively new experience for mankind. Real liberty for the individual only began with Christianity, and it was the full-flowering of Christian principles in America that made liberty happen here to an unprecedented degree.

"You Can't Hold a Good Man Down"

In the last chapter we learned that the plan of God cannot be thwarted, even by the most sophisticated "wrath of man." In the following pages we will historically trace the unleashing of the individual to fulfill God's plan, as the Christian idea of man and government gained dominance.

If you feel that each person has an "unalienable right" to life, liberty, and the fruit of his or her own labors, you share the Christian idea of man, which holds the individual as precious to God.

This idea of the uniqueness of the individual was completely foreign to the pagan ages of the world when the individual was submerged in his tribe or nation as a nameless, anonymous grain of sand. Even the Israelites had almost forgotten the God-created individual of Genesis I. What had happened to the individual and to the Dominion Mandate he had received from God?

What is the Dominion Mandate?

In Genesis I, Moses wrote down the story of creation. In the first four words of this book, God destroyed the religious foundation of polytheism. "In the beginning God..." At the very start, the Lord declares His sovereignty, pre-existence, and oneness. There are no other gods. He then proceeds to give His marching orders to His creature man:

> *"And God said, Let us make man in our image, after our likeness: and* let them have dominion *over the fish of the sea, and the fowl of the air, and over the cattle, and over all the earth, and over every creeping thing that creepeth upon the earth. So God created man in his own image, in the image of God created He him, male and female created he them. And God blessed them and God said unto them, Be fruitful and multiply, and replenish the earth, and subdue it, and* have dominion *over the fish of the sea, and over the fowl of the air, and over every living thing that moveth upon the earth."* (Gen. 1:26-28)

Notice that our orders were given in a specific sequence. First we must be fruitful and multiply and then replenish or fill the earth, and then we are to rule over the earth as God's sub-regents by subduing it, having dominion over all the earth.

Here, in the first words spoken to His highest creation, whom He created in His own image, God gives a world-engulfing commission to care for His creation. If this commission is still in force, then it will not allow us to escape our responsibility for the world's condition.

What About the Fall?

Was this great Dominion Mandate rescinded after the Fall? The Bible gives no evidence of such an assumption. In no way does God change His orders to His creation – except that man is condemned to earn his bread by the sweat of his brow and woman to bring forth her children in sorrow. But God does not give up the sovereignty of this world to Satan as some Biblical commentators have suggested. Quite the contrary, Satan is cursed and his assured defeat is promised through the death and resurrection of Christ (Gen.

3:14,15). We should also note that after the Fall, Cain and Abel offered the first fruits of their labor to God which has obvious reference to God's Dominion Mandate. By so doing, they were declaring God's ownership of the earth (Ex. 23:16; I Cor. 15:20) and their desire to be God's good stewards. And, in Gen. 4:20 and following, we also see men being named along with their vocations or commissions (such as cattlemen, musicians, brass and iron workers), illustrating the spreading of the mandate's application to every individual.

Again, after the Noahic flood, the Dominion Mandate is substantially repeated as the first words spoken to Noah when he left the Ark (Gen. 9:1-4). Do you think God is re-emphasizing the central importance of His Dominion Mandate in His plan for the individual? It would appear so.

Domination Replaces Dominion

Yet, just as the unique God-created individuality of men was lost sight of after the Fall, so was God's Dominion Mandate. Now man twisted the *dominion* God had given him over the earth into *domination* over his fellow man. Instead of obeying God's command to cultivate the earth, man proceeded to decimate it with endless wars to see who could be greatest. Men forgot the one God and bowed down to other gods of their own creating.

God's Covenant with a Man

The Jews alone continued to worship the one God and, through God's covenant with an individual, He blessed a nation. For God told Abraham that He would make a great nation from his seed and told him that "In thee shall all nations be blessed." (Gal. 3:8) It was God's intention that Abraham and his progeny would bring the pagan people back to God and restore a right relationship between the individual and his Lord.

To prepare His people for their task, He gave them His law, His prophets, and His very presence. But then, instead of following God's plan of self-government under His law, they demanded to be ruled by a King in order to be like all the pagan nations around them. (I Sam. 8) Instead of transforming the pagan world, they conformed to its view of man. Deaf to the warnings of their prophets, they were taken captive by a pagan people who had no respect for the individual. But during the darkest days of the Babylonian captivity, the prophet Jeremiah predicted that one day the Lord would write His law in the hearts of His people. (Jer. 31:33)

The Pagan Idea of Man

Despite the glorious promise of a New Covenant to come, Israel came ultimately under the yoke of the greatest pagan power of antiquity: Rome. As a fine American historian, Richard Frothingham, says of the pagan view of man that surrounded Israel:

"The individual was regarded as of value only as he formed a part of the political fabric, and was able to contribute to its uses, as though it were the end of his being to aggrandize the State. This was the pagan idea of man. The wisest philosophers of antiquity could not rise above it." (CHOC, p. 1)

The Greek philosopher, Plato, believed the State was of primary importance and the individual secondary. The "ideal" state in Plato's "Republic" was really a commune where family life was abolished and the entire focus of life was on serving the State. The communism he advocated was certainly inimical to individualism, as it is today. Communism is not the "wave of the future," but an ugly backlash from mankind's pagan past.

The State Becomes as God

Even Aristotle, whose wisdom is often quoted by early Church fathers, could not rise above this pagan idea that the state was of primary importance. (See Aristotle's Politics, Book I, Chapter 2) As Frothingham says:

"The State regarded as of paramount importance, not the man, but the citizen whose physical and intellectual forces it absorbed. If this tended to foster lofty civic virtues and splendid individual culture in the classes whom the State selected as the recipients of its favors, it bore hard on those whom the State virtually ignored, – on laboring men, mechanics, the poor, captives in war, slaves, and woman." (CHOC, pp. 1-2).

Despite the low view of the individual in both Greece and Rome, God had purposes for these pagan states. As the great traders and colonizers of the ancient world, the Greeks took their beautiful and rich language wherever they went, so that Greek was spoken everywhere. Here was the language that would articulate the Gospel to millions in succeeding centuries.

The Greeks were philosophers and artists, but the Romans were practical men – builders of great roads, public buildings, and temples to house their numerous gods. These Roman creations show the monolithic nature of Roman culture and the impersonal public nature of Roman life in which the State – majestic and all powerful – overshadowed the individual crushing him with its weight. (T&L, p. 163) The Romans also loved order and system and had a high degree of administrative ability. To a great extent, Rome succeeded in incorporating its conquered peoples into a national life, giving them the protection of its laws – something the old Oriental despotisms of Assyria and Persia had never done. (CHOC, pages 10-13)

"Christ Entered a Dying World"

When Christ appeared, these two civilizations were ready for His coming. God used these two national individualities in a remarkable way.

"When all parts of the civilized world were bound together in one empire – when one common organization pervaded the whole, – when channels of communication were everywhere opened – when new facilities of travelling were provided, – then was 'the fulness of time' (Gal. 4:4), then the Messiah came. The Greek language had already been prepared as a medium for preserving and transmitting the doctrine; the Roman government was now prepared to help the progress even of that religion which it persecuted." (T&L, p. 165)

There was great need for the Messiah to rescue mankind. Millions of nameless individuals were caught in the web of Roman despotism. There was nowhere to flee to get away from Rome's tyranny which embraced all the civilized world. The state of this world was grim: Greek civilization was now dead; what had been best in Rome had died with the Republic. All semblance of the impartial rule of Roman law was over as the Emperor Caesar Augustus gathered the reins of power into his own hands. He had ruled the Empire for 30 years when his decree "that all the world should be taxed" brought Mary and Joseph to Bethlehem. The Children of Israel were enslaved by the Romans and their religion was in decay. There had been no prophets in Israel for 400 years. Into this great darkness, God sent His Son. Swiss historian Philip Schaff says of this wondrous event:

"Christ entered a dying world as the author of a new and imperishable life."[1]

God revealed to men in the Old Testament their importance in His divine plan. As it is stated in Psalm 8:4-6, "What is man, that thou art mindful of him? and the son of man, that thou visitest him? For thou hast made him a little lower than the angels, and hast crowned him with glory and honour. Thou madest him to have dominion over the works of thy hands; thou has put all things under his feet."

Jesus restated God's initial and never-changing purpose for mankind by showing His love for each individual in the parable of the lost sheep. "What man of you, having an hundred sheep, if he lose one of them, doth not leave the ninety and nine in the wilderness, and go after that which is lost, until he find it? And when he hath found it, he layeth it on his shoulders, rejoicing. And when he cometh home, he calleth together his friends and neighbours, saying unto them, Rejoice with me; for I have found my sheep which was lost. I say unto you, that likewise joy shall be in heaven over one sinner that repenteth, more than over ninety and nine just persons, which need no repentance." (Luke 15:4-7)

A New Spirit and a New Power in the World

New life in Christ gave the individual a new value unknown in the ancient world or its religions. It began the work of transforming individual lives in the midst of the most pervasive tyranny the world had known, where the pagan idea of man reigned supreme. As Frothingham says:

> *"This low view of man was exerting its full influence when Rome was at the height of its power and glory. Christianity then appeared with its central doctrine, that man was created in the Divine image, and destined for immortality; pronouncing, that, in the eye of God, all men are equal. This asserted for the individual an independent value. It occasioned the great inference, that man is superior to the State, which ought to be fashioned for his use. This was the advent of a new spirit and a new power in the world."* (CHOC, p. 2)

God's plan of redemption was at last fulfilled in the Person of His Son, Jesus Christ, who brought a higher law to individuals everywhere, a law addressed to the individual heart, illumining rather than abolishing the Law of Moses.

Internal Liberty and External Freedom

"The Gospel brings forth a higher standard of liberty than *external law*," writes Christian educator, Rosalie J. Slater, for Christianity brings the *"internal law* of the Two Commandments of our Lord...it was not until the Saviour of mankind appeared that men learned that external freedom was achieved by internal liberty – 'the liberty wherewith Christ hath made us free.'" (T&L, p. 159)

The Gospel of Jesus Christ is addressed to the individual man, woman, and child; each is free to learn that, as Paul puts it, "I can do all things through Christ which strengtheneth me." (Phil. 4:13) Christ brings liberty to the individual – both religious and civil liberty.

Right of Individual Conscience Unknown

The right of individual conscience was inconceivable to the pagan mind. Rome was happy to adopt the gods of its conquered peoples; it was very tolerant of all nations' religious beliefs because they were *national* religions. But who had ever heard of individuals choosing their own religion? You were born into your religion; it was the religion of your fathers, of your nation. The Romans thought of Christianity simply as a Jewish heresy and a very dangerous one, for not only had these Christians deserted the religion of their fathers but they refused to bow down and worship the Emperor. They were not "reliable" citizens of the State. So the State persecuted them, until the Emperor Constantine adopted Christianity and made it the State religion in 312 A.D. Even before Constantine's adoption, however, the church had begun to lose its original self-governing nature. (See Chapter V – *God's World Changers*). Now the individual Christian lost the last vestiges of control that he had over his church, which began to borrow the hierarchical structure of the pagan Roman State.

The Reformation Recovers the Gospel

In the previous chapter, we have seen how the Reformation gave the Bible to the people, thus restoring to them their knowledge of the Gospel of Jesus Christ which had been kept in the hands of the priests. American historian Leonard Bacon says: "The great Reformation in the sixteenth century was an attempt to recover the primitive Gospel..." (CHOC, p. 20) It was also a demand for liberty of conscience for the individual Christian asserting his right to read the Scriptures and, by the aid of the indwelling Holy Spirit, to interpret them for himself. The Reformation "was the assertion of the principle of individuality, or of true spiritual freedom," says another historian. (CHOC, p. 1)

Separatists and Puritans

Roused by their growing knowledge of the Bible, which Henry VIII made it legal to read, many English Christians learned that the church in which they had grown up had strayed far from the original model in the New Testament. Many wished to reform the present national church. But, in addition to these Puritans, as they soon were called, were the men and women known as Separatists, the most famous of whom later became the Pilgrims.

"In the old world...the Puritan was a Nationalist, believing that a Christian nation is a Christian church, and demanding that the Church of England should be thoroughly reformed; while the Pilgrim was a Separatist...from all national churches...The Pilgrim wanted liberty for himself and his wife and little ones, and for his brethren, to walk with God in a Christian life as the rules and motives of such a life were revealed to him from God's Word" (CHOC, p. 182)

"Reformation Without Tarrying for Any"

A courageous young minister, Robert Browne, was thrown into prison repeatedly for preaching separation from the national church and the individual's "reformation without tarrying for any" and was finally forced to flee to Holland. But his words took hold of many who were still in England struggling with the great question: should I stay in the Church of England and try to reform it? Or, is the whole national church concept unscriptural?

In the little town of Scrooby in the north of England, "the idea of 'reformation without tarrying for any' was beginning to take effect..." (CHOC, p. 24) Here three individuals – future leaders of the Pilgrims – struggled with these questions.

Future Pilgrim Leaders

The church was built on the blood of the martyrs, as we have learned from the lives of great reformers like Wycliffe and Tyndale. These Christians were willing to pay the ultimate price for obeying God rather than man and for expressing their God-given individuality.

Through their work the stage was set for a fuller flowering of the individual. For this next great step, the most unlikely cast of characters was assembled – people without power, money or position. Nevertheless, they were to plant the seed of Christian liberty in a new world.

William Brewster

This remarkable Christian lived three lives – as confidential secretary to William Davison, a prominent member of Queen Elizabeth's court; then, after Davison's fall from favor, as a Separatist leader in England and Holland; finally, as the great spiritual leader of the Pilgrims in the Plymouth Colony.

After he returned from court to the quiet village of Scrooby, in East Anglia, he took over his ailing father's post as her Majesty's Postmaster and the Archbishop of York's Bailiff in charge of his estates in the area. He set about trying to reform the Church of England from within by getting good Scriptural preachers for the local churches and paying for them out of his own pocket. (Many churches went without preaching for years on end, since Queen Elizabeth plainly preferred the reading of government-approved "homilies" to sermons that reflected individual interpretation of Scripture.) When the Church of England demanded more rigid conformity to its rituals and rejected the right of individuals to hear "unauthorized" preachers, Brewster finally decided to separate from the Church and to covenant with other Christians in his area to form a Scriptural congregation.

> "...they shook off this yoake of antichristian bondage, and as ye Lord's free people, joyned themselves (by a covenant of the Lord) into a church estate, in ye fellowship of ye Gospell, to walke in all his wayes, made known or to be made known unto them, according to their best endeavours, whatsoever it should cost them, the Lord assisting them."
> (See CHOC, p. 185)

After the church was formed by covenant, Pilgrim historian William Bradford relates how Brewster "was a special stay and help unto them."[2]

> "They originally met at his house on the Lord's Day (which was a manor of the bishop's) and with great love he entertained them when they came, making provision for them to his great charge...And when they were to remove out of the country he was one of the first in all adventures..."[3]

71

Brewster bore all the ensuing trials in England, Holland, and America with unfailing resolution and good cheer. Later, when the Pilgrim Church was without a minister in the New World, he preached twice every Sunday and brought many to Christ. Bradford says that throughout his life Brewster was a highly effective evangelist. "He did more in this behalf in a year," the Pilgrim historian remarks, "than many...do in all their lives."[4]

John Robinson

Among others who participated in the covenant to form a Scriptural church was a young minister who had been dismissed from his first pastoral assignment for failure to conform to the Church of England's requirements regarding the wearing of priestly vestments. John Robinson hesitated long and prayed much over whether or not to withdraw from the national church. For a time he avoided the decision by trying to get a position as a preacher in a hospital in Norwich. Here he hoped to be allowed to conduct services where pure Christianity was preached. But his application was turned down and, with his wife and family, he returned to the Scrooby area to stay with relatives. His fine education at Cambridge University and his career in the church seemed now to count for nothing. Men could have said – and probably did – that he was a sad failure. But, instead, he was about to enter on his great life's work as pastor to the Pilgrims.

For some time Robinson was inwardly influenced by the example of those whom he respected who had remained in the Church of England. He blushed, he said, "to have a thought of pressing one hair-breadth before them in this thing, behind whom I knew myself to come so many miles in all other things." But the Holy Spirit would not let him alone. He says:

"..had not the truth been in my heart as a burning fire shut up in my bones, Jer. XX.9, I had never broken those bonds...wherein I was so straitly tied, but had suffered the light of God to have been put out in mine own unthankful heart by other men's darkness."[5]

But break the bonds he finally did and joined the Separatist congregation that met at Scrooby Manor. Though often neglected by historians, John Robinson should be known as one of the great Christian philosophers who propounded religious toleration in an intolerant age and representative government in an age of absolute monarchy. For twenty years, he taught these principles in depth to his persecuted and beloved Pilgrim church. More than any other man, John Robinson prepared a people to take dominion over a wilderness to the glory of God. Through his godly wisdom, he taught the Pilgrims individual Christian self-government and through the example of his Christian compassion, he taught them the value of Christian unity.

"His love was great towards them, and his care was all ways bente for their best good, both for soule and body; for besids his singuler abilities in devine things (wherein he excelled), he was also very able to give directions in civill affaires, and to foresee dangers & inconveniences; by which means he was very helpful to their outward estats, and so was every way as a commone father unto them...." (CHOC, p. 190)

William Bradford

Perhaps the greatest struggle for the right of individual conscience was that of young William Bradford of the nearby village of Austerfield. Orphaned when only a small child, he was raised first by his grandfather and then by his uncles who trained him to be a farmer. During a long childhood illness, Bradford began to read the Bible seriously. When he was a teenager, another boy took him to the church at Babworth to hear the Rev. Richard Clyfton preach. Young Bradford was so impressed with Clyfton's Scriptural preaching that he continued attending the Babworth church until Clyfton withdrew to become minister of the small Separatist congregation at Scrooby. Despite enormous pressure upon him to remain in the Church of England, young Bradford decided:

"to withdraw from the communion of the parish-assemblies, and engage with some society of the faithful that should keep close unto the written word of God, as the rule of their worship...although the provoked rage of his friends tried all the ways imaginable to reclaim him from it, unto all...his answer was...'Nevertheless, to keep a good conscience, and walk in such a way as God has prescribed in his word, is a thing which I must prefer before you all, and above life itself.'"[6]

When Bradford started attending the small Separatist church that met at Scrooby Manor, he found a father in William Brewster who shared his fine Cambridge education with the talented youth. Bradford was to become not only an outstanding Pilgrim leader in the New World, serving as the governor of the Plymouth Colony for 33 years, but also the author of the *History of Plymouth Plantation*. In this account of the Pilgrims, Bradford produced the first great literary work written on these shores.

These three individuals — a village postmaster, an obscure clergyman, and a young farmer lad — little dreamed of the marvelous ways in which God would use them in the succeeding years. But they had heeded Paul's admonition: "Be not conformed to this world: but be ye transformed by the renewing of your mind, that ye may prove what is that good, and acceptable, and perfect, will of God." (Rom. 12:2) Renewed and transformed by God, their joy was great as was their love for each other. But soon these transformed Christians were persecuted severely for refusing to conform to the Church of England. (See CHOC, p. 185)

Beginnings of Self-Government

In 1608, they succeeded in reaching Holland after many harrowing adventures in their first two abortive attempts to flee from England. In Holland, they found toleration, although not full religious liberty; here their pastor, John Robinson, instructed them in the Scriptures; and here they forged strong bonds of Christian fellowship and learned to be a self-governing people. But after 12 years in Holland, they were guided by God to leave that land for the wilderness of America.

In the next chapter we shall see the foundation they laid for Christian civil government in the New World. Among the Pilgrims, we find many other important foundations. As Rosalie J. Slater points out:

> "In the record of Plymouth Colony we find the parenthood of our Republic. Here can be found the seed of all our important institutions. Here begins our precious record of Christian Character, Christian Self-Government, Christian Economics, Christian Education, and Biblical Christian Unity. For it is what constitutes the character of individual Americans that determines whether our government, economics, education and unity are Christian or pagan." (T&L, p. 178).

For these reasons, we shall be referring often to this small band of dedicated Christians who illustrate so vividly what the individual can do when he has been set free by Christ.

Christian Individuality
Vs.
Humanistic Individualism

The individuality typified by the Pilgrims however, was not the "do your own thing" sort of humanistic individualism so prevalent today.

Humanistic individualism implies a man-centered universe with no moral absolutes to control man and is an invitation to anarchy.

Christian individuality implies a God-centered universe with the individual controlled by God's laws and is an invitation to enjoy Christ's Law of Liberty within the bounds of His unchanging order.

As we go back and view our origins from the Christian perspective – as we recover our lost heritage of Christian principles – we shall be equipped as never before to go *forward* as world-transforming Christians – beginning with ourselves, then our families, churches, schools, communities, states, and our nation.

Today, there are many signs that a revival of respect for the individual's God-given rights is impacting world events. In America, our President is calling for a renewed emphasis upon individual enterprise and self-government which he perceptively sees as the genius of the American people. Many Americans are becoming increasingly concerned about the rights of the unborn individual, the handicapped, and the aged.

Behind the Iron and Bamboo curtains, Bibles are being read and men are realizing, like our Pilgrim Fathers, their significance before God as individuals who are not destined to be the chattel of the state. The Polish people, in their quest for individual and economic freedom are an example of a people who, after 35 years of brainwashing, have not forgotten the sovereignty of God over the state.

The Russian communists know that the Christian faith is their Achilles' heel. They have tried to annihilate its truth but to no avail. Their empire continues to self-destruct, but the underground church grows and perseveres.

Unfortunately, Americans for the most part have forgotten the power of the individual and his Biblical view of man and government, a power that undermines tyranny and brings liberty to cultures that are in bondage. We, as our Pilgrim Fathers, need to see that the wordly power and position of the individual do not determine his world-changing capability. An American individual, burdened with taxation and struggling to raise a family, often questions whether one lone voice can ever be heard, whether it is worth trying to change the depressing status quo. Only the providential view of history, which guided the Pilgrims, can give the individual hope that an all-powerful God can open doors that men have closed, can use the individual to accomplish great things. When we see ourselves as God sees us, as His sub-regents (Rev. 1:6) and Dominion men and women (Gen. 1:26-28), we become God's world-changers.

Notes:

1. Philip Schaff, *History of the Christian Church*, 8 vols. (Grand Rapids, Michigan: Wm. B. Eerdmans Publishing Co., 1978), I, p. 59.
2. William Bradford, *Of Plymouth Plantation: 1620-1647*, ed. Samuel Eliot Morison, The Modern Library (Random House, Inc., 1967), p. 326.
3. Ibid.,
4. Ibid., p. 327.
5. John Brown, *The Pilgrim Fathers of New England and Their Puritan Successors* (Pasadena, Texas: Pilgrim Publications, 1970), p. 93.
6. Cotton Mather, *Life of William Bradford* in *The Story of the Pilgrim Fathers* (London: Ward and Downey, 1897; Boston and New York: Houghton, Mifflin & Co., 1897; New York: Klaus Reprint Co., 1969), p. 40.

Further Reading – Chapter 4

Chapter 4 – Study Questions

1. Why is the individual important? _____

_____

_____

2. What is entailed in the Dominion Mandate? What does it include – and what does it *not* include? _____

_____

_____

3. What was the pagan idea of man and government? _____
_____
_____

4. Why did the pagan civilizations of Greece and Rome make the state paramount in their system and man secondary? _____
_____
_____

5. Why does the "inward law" brought by Jesus Christ help us to fulfill the "outward law" of Moses? _____
_____
_____

6. What was the Reformation in its essence? _____
_____
_____

7. Do we need reformation today? In what ways? _____
_____
_____

8. What happens when individualism is divorced from Christianity? What effects does it produce? _____
_____
_____

9. What happens to the relations between individuals in a man-centered, rather than God-centered, universe? _____
_____
_____

10. Do we Christians today think of ourselves primarily as individuals, or do we think of ourselves primarily as members of groups – religious, economic, and social? _____
_____
_____

11. Are Christians persecuted today? By Whom? Why? _____
_____
_____

12. Why is religious persecution always wrong? _____
_____
_____

13. In America, what is to keep any one Christian denomination from persecuting other churches or unbelievers? _____
_____
_____

Chapter 5

God's World-Changers

"Stand fast therefore in the liberty wherewith Christ hath made us free, and be not entangled again with the yoke of bondage."

Galatians 5:1

GOV. WINTHROP ARRIVES AT SALEM ON THE ARBELLA (1630)

"Thus stands the cause between God and us, we are entered into Covenant with Him for this worke...Now if the Lord shall please to bear us, and bring us in peace to the place we desire, then hath He verified this Covenant and sealed our Commission...."

— John Winthrop in ''Christian Charitie:
A Modell Thereof.''

Chapter 5

God's World-Changers

Many Americans today question the assertion that the self-governing Christian is a world-changer. Perhaps the average church-goer they know does not appear to be transforming society.

Yet, in Scripture, the Christian is seen as more than a man who does good and avoids evil. He has within him, because of his faith in Christ, all the power to subdue God's earth to His glory.

Throughout this guide we speak of this revolutionary individual as the self-governing Christian. Before we give an historical survey of the impact of God's world-changers, let us begin by defining self-government.

Today in America our tendency is to think of the word "government" in purely external terms: as "they" – the people in city hall, statehouse, or Washington, D.C. To us they are the "government." So, at first the term self-government seems strange. If it is used in a humanistic sense – suggesting that every man is free to govern himself however he wishes without reference to God's moral law – then self-government becomes anarchy. The meaning of the word "self-government" as our Founders understood it can only be grasped when we are willing to be governed by the Scriptures.

Christ's Internal Government

Christ's government is internal, resulting in the Christian being self-governing, but always in accord with God's laws. Self-government that ignores God's laws or defies them is not true self-government and leads not to liberty, but to the bondage Jesus refers to in John 8:34: "Whosoever committeth sin is the servant of sin." Only when the Son shall set you free are you free indeed. (John 8:36)

Pilgrim Self-Government

The Pilgrims clearly understood the *source* of their self-government. A passage on self-government from Scripture that they must have heeded well is: "For if a man know not how to rule his own house, how shall he take care of the Church of God?" (I Tim. 3:5)

As soon as the Pilgrims settled in their Dutch haven in the city of Leyden, the question of caring for the Church of God was much on their mind. Here, in hospitable Holland, the Pilgrims entered into the important second stage of their development as self-governing Christians, a stage which had just begun in England. It was now their task to establish firmly their new self-governing church. For guidance, they turned to the New Testament model.

Spontaneous Associations

They discovered that the New Testament churches were spontaneous associations of believers: "Individuals and families, drawn toward each other by their common trust in Jesus the Christ...became a community united, not by external bonds, but by the vital force of distinctive ideas and principles." (CHOC, p. 16)

They also discovered that the organization of the church at Jerusalem was "essentially democratic" and, indeed, "in every place the society of believers in Christ was a little republic..." So, in common with all Separatist churches which had similarly studied the New Testament, the Pilgrims set up a congregational form of government whereby they governed themselves through elected officers. Their sworn enemy was the corrupted Church of England and its tyrannical centralized Episcopacy which was, in turn, controlled by the Crown. Studying the Bible, they discovered how this had come about.

The Church Corrupted

The self-governing Christians of the New Testament churches had only delegated their powers to their church officers to conduct the business of the Church. But, under pressure of persecution in the days before Constantine adopted Christianity, they gradually granted more and more "emergency powers" to their leaders. By 300 A.D., the church had adopted a centralized Episcopal form of government, although their Bishops were still democratically elected by the congregations.

There are many lessons for us today in what happened to the self-government of God's people at this time. (See CHOC, p. 19) The importance of knowing our history is underlined by the fact that the early Christians let their powers of self-government slip away from them because, unlike us today, they had no experience to guide them. "Why should they be jealous for their liberty? How should they be expected to detect and resist the beginning of lordship over God's heritage?" (CHOC, p. 19)

But when Constantine adopted Christianity as the state religion in 312 A.D., the self-governing Christian soon lost the last vestiges of control over his church. It was no longer the spontaneous, self-governing association of believers, but a hierarchical structure with power at the top dictating its will to the people below.

The One, the Few, and the Many

The Pilgrims had suffered severely enough from a State-controlled Episcopacy to know it was not in accord with Christ's Law of Liberty. Their beloved pastor, John Robinson, wrote down his thoughts on the three basic forms of government known to the world. He concluded that all three forms had their place in the church of Christ:

> "...monarchical, where supreme authority is in the hands of the one, aristocratical when it is in the hands of some few...and democratical, in the whole body or multitude...In respect of Him the head, it is a monarchy, in respect of the eldership, an aristocracy, in respect of the body, a popular state...the Lord Jesus is the King of his church above, upon whose shoulders the government is, and unto whom all power is given in heaven and earth...But Christ has committed this power to the church annointing all men as "Kings and Priests unto God" (Rev. 1:6)[1]

In Christ's church, Robinson maintained, each member functioned as a King by guiding and governing himself – "in the ways of godliness" and as a Priest by offering up "prayers, praises, and thanksgiving" – but all in accord with "those special determinations which the Lord Jesus, the King of Kings hath prescribed." Even the least member of the body of Christ "hath received his drop...of this anointing, so is not to be despised."

Robinson then dealt with the question of how a congregation of kings and priests could all govern without ensuing chaos!

> "...someone or few must needs be appointed over the assembly [for]...discussing and determining of all matters, so in this royal assem-

bly, the church of Christ, though all be Kings, yet some most faithful and most able, are to be set over the rest...wherein...they are...charged to minister according to the Testament of Christ." [2]

But, Robinson warned, this government by elected representatives did not involve any lordship over God's people, for these representatives were but to serve their brothers and sisters in Christ, "affording the Lord and them their best service."[3] This is confirmed by the Scriptures in I Pet. 5:3 where the elders are exhorted not to be lords over God's heritage but to be examples to the flock.

This was the structure of the Pilgrim church under Pastor Robinson's inspired leadership: Christ the King giving to each one self-government; then the Christians, forming the Body of Christ, electing representatives from among themselves to carry on the work of the church. By the time the truce between Holland and Spain was drawing to a close and war clouds were gathering, the Pilgrims were well grounded in Christian self-government in relation to themselves and their church and ready to take on the challenge of the next step in God's plan for them.

Protracted negotiations with the Virginia Company of London for a patent to plant a colony in America were discouraging to many of the Pilgrims and, in the end, it was only a small number of Robinson's congregation who were willing to be among the first to go. Robinson decided, reluctantly, that he must stay behind with the greater number. Meanwhile, Elder William Brewster would accompany the Pilgrims to America and minister to their spiritual needs.

The Floating Republic

Less than half of the 102 passengers on the Mayflower were Pilgrims. The rest had been recruited by the "Merchant Adventurers" who helped finance the venture. Some of these "strangers" were to become excellent citizens of the new colony, but others were dishonest troublemakers who caused many difficulties.

Wisely foreseeing how greatly their capacities for self-government would be tested, Pastor Robinson wrote the Pilgrims a farewell letter containing much useful counsel on self-government. He urged them first of all to renew their repentance with God daily and after this "peace with God" and their own consciences, "carefully to provide for peace with all men," and neither to give offence "nor easily to take offence being given by others." He knew that because many of the travelers were strangers to the Pilgrims, the Pilgrims would "stand in need of more watchfulness this way, lest when such things fall out in men and women as you suspected not, you be inordinately affected with them...." (CHOC, pp. 198-199)

The Pilgrim Body Politic

Then, moving from Christian self-government to the sphere of Christian civil government, Robinson wrote:

"Lastly, whereas you are become a body politic, using amongst yourselves civil government, let your wisdom and godliness appear not only in choosing such persons as do entirely love and will promote the common good, but also in yielding unto them all due honor and obedience in their lawful administrations; not beholding in them the ordinariness of their persons, but God's ordinance for your good..." (CHOC, p. 200)

In the prayer concluding his letter, he asked the Lord to guide them "inwardly by his Spirit, so outwardly by the hand of his power." (CHOC, p. 201) God did, indeed, guide them through the perilous voyage. His providential hand saved their lives in miraculous ways from the fury of the storms which battered the Mayflower and he brought them safely to His destination for them. Then He gave them the wisdom to see what needed to be done to quell the mutinous murmurs of some of the "strangers" on board who, as Bradford relates, said that when they got ashore "they would use their own liberties; for none had power to command them, the patent they had being for Virginia and not for New England..." (CHOC, p. 204)

America's Founding Covenant: The Mayflower Compact

Because of these "discontented and mutinous speeches," the Pilgrim leaders, Deacon Carver, Elder Brewster, and the young William Bradford, realized that their civil government would have to be placed on a firm Christian base before leaving the ship or a state of anarchy would set in. The Pilgrims accomplished this in their vitally-important document, *The Mayflower Compact.*

"In ye name of God, Amen. We whose names are underwritten, the loyall subjects of our dread soveraigne Lord, King James, by ye grace of God, of Great Britaine, France, & Ireland king, defender of ye faith, &c., having undertaken, for ye glorie of God, and advancement of ye Christian faith, and honour of our king & countrie, a voyage to plant ye first colonie in ye Northerne parts of Virginia, doe by these presents solemnly & mutually in ye presence of God, and one of another, covenant & combine our selves togeather into a civill body politick, for our better ordering & preservation & furtherance of ye ends aforesaid; and by vertue hearof to enacte, constitute, and frame such just & equall lawes, ordinances, acts, constitutions & offices, from time to time, as shall be thought most meete & convenient for ye generall good of ye Colonie, unto which we promise all due submission and obedience. In witness wherof we have hereunder subscribed our names at Cap-Codd ye 11. of November, in ye year of ye raigne of our soveraigne lord, King James, of England, France, & Ireland ye eighteenth, and of Scotland ye fiftie fourth. Ano:Dom. 1620." (CHOC, p. 204)

This was to be the first of many such "plantation covenants" as they were called to distinguish them from "church covenants." These plantation covenants form one of the pillars of American constitutional government.

In discussing the Mayflower Compact, Professor Andrew McLaughlin, a leading scholar in the field of American Constitutional history, says that "it is impossible...to neglect the word 'covenant,' and not see in the compact the transmutation of a church covenant into the practical foundation of a self-governing community."[4]

Communal Farming Fails

In the difficult days that lay ahead, the Christian character and self-government the Pilgrims had learned and the strong bonds of Christian fellowship forged at Scrooby and tested in Holland stood them in good stead. After the first disastrous winter in which more than half of them died, amazingly none of the survivors returned to England when the Mayflower finally left for the Mother Country. But the little colony nearly foundered because of the collective economic system the merchants in London had foisted on it, all the settlers working only for the joint partnership and being fed out of the common stores. The land, too, and the houses they built on it were to be the joint property of the merchants and colonists for seven years and then divided equally. On the death of Deacon Carver who had been the Pilgrim governor, young William Bradford, then only 30 years old, was elected their new Governor and soon proved the high quality of his leadership.

The agreement with the merchants had caused much resentment among Pilgrims and "strangers" alike and reduced productivity. Finally, Bradford saw that bold, decisive action was needed. As he wrote later in his History:

> "...after much debate of things, the Governor (with the advice of the chiefest amongst them) gave way that they should set corn every man for his own particular, and in that regard trust to themselves..." (CHOC, p. 213)

Free-Enterprise Flourishes

Bradford assigned a plot of land to each family to work. "This had very good success; for it made all hands very industrious..." he wrote. From then on, there was never a famine at Plymouth.

Bradford's comments on this event are signficant.

> "The experience that was had in this common course and condition, tried sundry years, and that amongst godly and sober men, may well evince the vanity and conceit of Plato and other ancients... – that the taking away of property, and bringing in community [communism] into a commonwealth, would make them happy and flourishing; as if they were wiser than God. For this community...was found to breed much confusion and discontent, and retard much imployment that would have been to their benefit and comfort." (CHOC, p. 213)

As Rosalie J. Slater remarks of the abundant harvest that resulted from Governor Bradford's decision to establish individual enterprise: "The opportunity to 'work out your own salvation' challenged Christian self-government – the desire and ability of each individual to work to his fullest capacity." (T&L, p. 196)

This experience was in sharp contrast to what happened in the Virginia Colony. Both colonies were planted to the glory of God, The Virginia Colony's charter, like the Mayflower Compact, makes this abundantly clear.

> "We greatly commend and graciously accept their desires for the furtherance of so noble a work, which may, by the providence of Almighty God, hereafter tend to the glory of His Divine Majesty, in propagating of

Christian religion to such people as yet live in darkness and miserable ignorance of the true knowledge and worship of God...."

Many of the early settlers at Jamestown, however, were soldiers of fortune intent on mere economic gain. Moreover, they went to Virginia without their families and with no intentions of settling there permanently. The desire for *external* gain – to find and seize the gold and pearls the Indians were rumored to possess – was in sharp contrast to the Pilgrim's desire to found their colony for *internal* liberty of conscience.

The Leaven of Liberty

Although it never became a large colony and was later absorbed by its neighbor, the Massachusetts Bay Colony, Plymouth exercised a profound influence on Massachusetts and the other colonies that developed later in Connecticut and Rhode Island.

The colony of Salem had started out to plant a Puritan branch of the Church of England in the New World, but it was not long before the colonists began to have different views of church government. (See CHOC, pp. 241-244) The leader of the Salem colonists, John Endicott, was deeply impressed by the Separatists at Plymouth. Governor Bradford had sent the Pilgrims' physician, Deacon Fuller, to help the Salem people when they suffered from a terrible epidemic in 1628. Fuller labored to heal their sick and then before returning to Plymouth, he took time to correct some of Endicott's misconceptions about the Separatists. Endicott sent a warm letter of thanks to Governor Bradford for all that Fuller had done to help them and mentioned how glad he was to have learned about their religious views. Soon after, in 1629, Endicott took the lead in effecting a remarkable change.

He and the other Puritans at Salem decided that – unlike the Church of England which accepted everyone within its territory – their church would only include those who had made a profession of faith. To this end, one of their ministers drew up a statement for those joining the church "solemnly to enter into a covenant engagement one with another, in the presence of God, to walk together before him according to his Word."[5]

Governor Bradford and William Brewster from Plymouth were invited to the special day set aside for the forming of the new church. Although the voyage across the bay was delayed by headwinds so that they arrived too late to afford the Salem congregation their "direction and assistance," they had the joy of learning that the new church had been formed, as theirs had been, by covenanting with the Lord, and that the people had freely elected their own church officers.

"The church that had been brought over the ocean now saw another church, the first-born in America, holding the same faith in the same simplicity of self-government under Christ alone." [6]

The Great Puritan Exodus

By 1630 the great Puritan exodus from England was under way. Renewed persecution by Charles I and Archbishop Laud gave a strong impetus to the desire many Puritans had long cherished of quitting England for a land where they could worship God in accord with the Scriptures. The new colonists who arrived on the New England coast in 1630, unlike the Pilgrims, were men of means. "Some of them came from stately homes and were possessed of wealth and social position," historian John Brown points out, "while others had occupied influential positions as ministers of the Church." [7] During the remainder of Charles I's reign, England was drained of some of its best intellects and a great deal of money.

> *"Upon the whole it has been computed that the four settlements of New England, viz. Plymouth, the Massachussets Bay, Connecticut, and New Haven...drained England of four or five hundred thousand pounds in money (a very great sum in those days); and if the persecution of the Puritans had continued twelve years longer, it is thought that a fourth part of the riches of the kingdom would have passed out of it through this channel."* (CHOC, p. 181)

But these men who, in 1629, were preparing to establish a new colony in New England were unwilling to do so if the Massachusetts Bay Company remained merely a commercial trading body headquartered in London and subject to interference from the King. But how could they hope to set up a colony that would not be controlled by the home government? As they prayed about this, Divine Providence provided a way.

In March 1629, a Royal Charter was granted to the Company creating a new corporation. The Charter specified that a governor, deputy governor and 18 assistants would be empowered to make all reasonable laws for the colony. But the question of *where* these officers would hold their meetings was simply not mentioned in the charter and – providentially – the autocratic King Charles did not notice this glaring omission and signed the charter! This was done the same week he dissolved Parliament and vowed to rule England alone. Thus, while annihilating representative government in England with one hand, with the other he unwittingly created a self-governing colony in America! In July 1629, the Massachusetts Bay Company simply voted to transfer the government of the plantation from England to the new colony. This allowed it to establish an independent, self-governing colony where, like their Pilgrim neighbors, they could worship the Lord according to the dictates of their conscience.

> *"From the point of view of our later age, the removal of the charter government to America is the event of chief importance in this migration....The ultimate effect of this brilliant stroke was so to modify a commercial corporation that it became a colonial government as independent as possible of control from England. By the admission of a large number of colonists to be freemen – that is, to vote as stockholders in the affairs of the company, which was now the colony itself, and a little later by the development of a second chamber – the government became representative..."* (CHOC, p. 180)

The Moses of a New Exodus

On March 23, 1630, some 1,000 Puritans embarked for New England on four well-provisioned ships. Arranging such an expedition had been an enormous burden, but in John Winthrop the Company found a man who was fully equal to the task. "He was a man of remarkable strength and beauty of character," writes John Fiske. "When his life shall have been adequately written...he will be recognized as one of the very noblest figures in American history."[8]

> *"From early youth he had that same power of winning confidence and commanding respect for which Washington was so remarkable; and when he was selected as the Moses of the great Puritan exodus, there was a wide-spread feeling that extraordinary results were likely to come of such an enterprise."*[9]

The son of a prosperous country lawyer from Suffolk, Winthrop had followed his father's footsteps into a career in the law and gave up a lucrative position as Attorney in the Court of Wards in order to emigrate to New England. He was to deplete his estate in Suffolk substantially in order to help sustain the Bay Colony in its early years.

"Christian Charitie: A Modell Thereof"

While at sea on board the flagship, the *Arbella*, this thoughtful, self-sacrificing Christian leader wrote an important paper known today as "A Model of Christian Charity," which he shared with his fellow Puritans. It is an eloquent statement of their motives and goals for the new colony. First of all, Winthrop wished them to remember *who* they were. "...we are a company, professing our selves fellow members of Christ knit together by this bond of love," he tells them. And *what* was to be their purpose? He writes that the work they had in hand was to seek a place to live together "under a due form of government, both civill and ecclesiastical..." But theirs was not to be a mere legal agreement. As in the Mayflower Compact, their relationship to God and to each other is described in covenantal terms:

> *"Thus stands the cause between God and us, we are entered into Covenant with Him for this worke...Now if the Lord shall please to bear us, and bring us in peace to the place we desire, then hath he verified this Covenant and sealed our Commission...."*[10]

"A City Upon a Hill"

With a clear vision of their place in history, Winthrop prayed that God "...shall make us a praise and glory, that men shall say of succeeding plantations: the Lord make it like that of New England for we must consider we shall be as a city upon a hill, the eyes of all people are upon us; so that if we shall deal falsely with our God in this work we have undertaken and so cause Him to withdraw his present help from us, we shall be made a story and a byword through the world...."[12]

What a reminder to twentieth century American Christians of our duty and what a solemn warning! Are not the eyes of the world, as well as the eyes of God, focused upon America today, critically evaluating how well we are living out the principles of our founding covenants?

The Puritans Cling to a State Church

The great desire of the Puritan was to be self-governing in accord with God's laws. But the Puritan's zeal and strength of character needed to be tempered with Pilgrim compassion. This tempering process had already begun with Deacon Fuller's visit to Salem. Historian Edward Eggleson notes that *"the Church discipline and the form of government in Massachusetts borrowed much from Plymouth, but the mildness and semi-toleration – the 'toleration of tolerable opinions" – which Robinson had impressed on the Pilgrims was not so easily communicated to their new neighbors who had been trained in another school."* (CHOC, p. 244)

The Puritans wanted a self-governing colony – but one in which political power remained in the hands of their fellow Puritans. They still clung to a state church.

How Much Self-Government?

The arrival of the *Arbella* and her sister ships was followed by many more vessels from England bringing new settlers. Soon, Boston was established and other settlements sprang up all over Massachusetts Bay. These towns followed Salem's lead in establishing their churches by covenant in emulation of their Pilgrim neighbors. But the Puritans continued to disavow Separatism. They still considered themselves members of the Church of England but now liberated from its corruptions. While they were united with regard to their church government, there soon was conflict concerning the colony's civil government. It had been intended originally that the freemen elect the governor, deputy governor and the assistants. But as early as October 1630 an attempt was made to transfer power from the freemen to the governor, deputy governor and assistants, and a proposal was made that the governor be elected – not by the freemen – but by the assistants! When the government in Boston attempted to levy a special tax for frontier fortifications against a possible attack by the French, strong objections were raised by colonists in outlying settlements. They pointed out that according to English law they could not be taxed except with their own consent. They insisted that the power to tax lay with the whole body of the people, that is, with the freemen of the colony. The Boston elite backed down and all the freemen were allowed to elect the governor, deputy governor and assistants.

"There was also an extension of self-government in the arrangement that every town should send two representatives to advise the governor and assistants on the question of taxation."[12]

92

The Puritan Theocracy

The latter was certainly a step toward liberty. But, in 1631, it was partially counteracted by a decision that "no man shall be admitted to the freedom of this body politic, but such as are members of some of the churches within the limits of the same."[13] This provision that none but church members could vote or hold office narrowed the franchise considerably and did not set well with many people. Why, they asked, should non-church members be disenfranchised and yet still be obliged to fulfill their civic duties? Why should they have no say in regard to making or executing the laws that were to govern them and for which they paid taxes!

Another Kind Of Puritan

One of those to object was a remarkable Puritan pastor from Essex, England, who arrived in the Bay Colony in 1633. The Rev. Thomas Hooker was a learned man who (like so many other Puritans) had been educated at Cambridge University and had become one of England's most eloquent supporters of Scriptural Christianity. Unfortunately, he was so eloquent that he attracted the attention of Laud, the Archbishop of Cantebury. Learning that Laud was planning to arrest him, Rev. Hooker escaped to Holland in 1630. Here he lived for three years until he felt that the Lord was calling him to go to New England.

Soon after his arrival in the Bay Colony, Hooker became pastor of the church at Newtown (now Cambridge). He had not long been in the colony when he became disturbed concerning the question of restricted voting rights about which he wrote to John Winthrop, now Governor Winthrop, who replied to him that "the best part is always the least, and of that best part the wiser part is always the lesser."[14] Great as he was as a conscientious Bible-believing Christian leader, Winthrop could not transcend the elitist outlook of the Puritan aristocracy. But Rev. Hooker could not concur with his views and replied that "in matters which concern the common good, a general council, chosen by all, to transact businesses which concern all, I conceive most suitable to rule and most safe for relief of the whole."[15]

Nor could he agree with Winthrop that the assistants need not be elected annually, but for good behaviour, that is, for life – unless guilty of some serious misdeed! Later, Hooker was to write to Winthrop:

"I must confess, I ever looked at it, as a way which leads to tyranny and so to confusion, and must plainly profess, if it was in my liberty, I should choose neither to live, nor leave my posterity, under such a government."[16]

Another Great Migration

But Governor Winthrop and the Boston Puritans were adamant. So, in June 1636, Rev. Thomas Hooker and his congregation at Newtown – some 100 people – left the Massachusetts Bay Colony to settle in the Connecticut Valley. They were followed by the congregations of Dorchester and Watertown. By May 1637, 800 people had moved from the Boston area to populate Windsor, Wethersfield and Hartford. So, the Bay Colony lost not just a few individuals, but virtually three whole towns in this dispute over self-government.

For a year these Connecticut towns consented to be governed by a Board of Commissioners from Massachusetts, but then they assembled together and elected their own representatives in a General Court held in Hartford in 1638. For many years, historians did not know the critical role Thomas Hooker played in producing the new government and its landmark constitution. But in the middle of the nineteenth century, a little volume was found in Windsor in which someone had transcribed notes in cipher on sermons and lectures given by Rev. Thomas Hooker and other ministers. In this volume was discovered a digest of the remarkable, statesmanlike sermon Hooker gave before the General Court on May 31, 1638.

The Foundation of Authority

Taking Deut. 1:13 as his text, "Take you wise men and understanding...and I will make them rulers over you," he told the people that "the foundation of authority is laid...in the free consent of the people" and that "the choice of public magistrates belongs unto the people by God's own allowance," that they who have the power to appoint officers and magistrates have the right also "to set the bounds and limitations of the power and place unto which they call them." (CHOC, pp. 250-251)

The various points Rev. Hooker enumerated in his sermon formed the basis of the Fundamental Orders of Connecticut which were adopted as the Constitution of Connecticut by the freemen of the three towns assembled in Hartford on January 14, 1639.

January 14, 1639

In the *Fundamental Orders of Connecticut,* we have a document that is far ahead of its time in recognizing the origin of all civil government as derived from God and "the agreement and covenant of the whole body of the governed." Here the American Covenant, begun by the Mayflower Compact, developed into a full-fledged body of laws.

"It was the first written constitution known to history, that created a government, and it marked the beginnings of American democracy, of which Thomas Hooker deserves more than any other man to be called the father." (CHOC, p. 252)

Not only is this so, but to historian Fiske the government of the United States is "in lineal descent more nearly related to that of Connecticut than to any of the other thirteen colonies."

"The most noteworthy features of the Connecticut republic was that it was a federation of independent towns and that all attributes of sovereignty not expressly granted to the General Court remained, as of original right, in the towns..." (CHOC, p. 252)

Here, in the Fundamental Orders, is a microcosm of the Federal Constitution to come.

A Distinct Departure

Significantly, the Fundamental Orders did not require church membership in order to vote or hold most offices. (An exception was the governor who was to be a member of "some approved congregation." See CHOC, p. 254) This was a distinct departure from the Puritan view of civil government as a theocracy which, in practice, meant rule of the state by a specific Christian denomination with its specific interpretation of Scripture. But it was in no way an attempt to secularize the state or separate it from Biblical law. On the contrary, the document reflected the sincere *Biblical consensus* of the people. It acknowledged that wherever a people are gathered together, the Word of God requires them to set up "an orderly and decent government established according to God." (CHOC, p. 253) Thus did they "enter into combination and confederation together to maintain and preserve the liberty and purity of the gospel of our Lord Jesus Christ." (CHOC, p. 253)

A Strong Political Structure

Providentially, this little federal republic grew until, "it became the strongest political structure on the continent, as was illustrated in the remarkable military energy and the unshaken financial credit of Connecticut during the Revolutionary War..." (CHOC, p. 242) It was Connecticut, too, that broke the deadlock at the Constitutional Convention of 1787 with its compromise by which it was decided that the states be represented equally in the Senate but on the basis of population in the House of Representatives.

What great steps forward in the art of Christian self-government were taken as the result of one New England minister's vision sustained by Divine Providence!

Roger Williams Demands Liberty of Conscience

The hand of God may also be seen in the founding of the colony called Providence where full religious liberty was at last achieved. When young Separatist Roger Williams arrived in the Bay Colony in 1631, a refugee from the tyranny of Charles I, he refused a post as a teacher in the church of Boston because it would not renounce all fellowship with the Church of England. An eloquent, inspiring preacher, warm-hearted and earnest, Williams served as Minister at Plymouth and then at Salem.

His uncompromising views, however, in regard to having any dealings with the Church of England caused much controversy. When he advanced the argument that the King of England had no title to land held by the Indians and therefore no authority to issue the charter under which the Massachusetts Puritans were trying to enforce religious uniformity on everyone, he really ran into trouble. His demand for liberty of conscience for the self-governing Christian resulted in his trial and banishment from the Bay Colony in 1635. Driven into the wilderness, he purchased land from the Indians and founded Providence which soon attracted many who had been persecuted for their religious convictions.

The settlers under Roger Williams at Providence entered into a written covenant providing obedience *"to all such orders and agreements as shall be made for public good of the body in an orderly way, by the major consent of the present inhabitants...incorporated together in a Towne fellowship..."*[17] Thus the banishment of Roger Williams from Massachusetts resulted in the establishment of liberty of conscience in the colony of Providence. Once again, God used "the wrath of men to praise Him" (Psalm 76:10) and bring about another step in the development of Christian self-government.

Self-Governing Baptists

In 1639, Baptists, who like the Separatists, believed in self-governing churches and were strongly opposed to any national church, began to take refuge at Providence. Pastor Williams was impressed with their doctrine that only adult, and not infant, baptism was Scriptural. He was baptized and helped to found at Providence the First Baptist Church in America. Although he did not remain a Baptist for long, feeling continually driven to seek "a purer form of Christianity," his impassioned stand for liberty of conscience enabled the Baptists and other dissenters to have the freedom to develop their own self-governing churches in accord with individual Christian conscience.

The Body of Liberties

Meanwhile, the colonists in Massachusetts Bay were becoming increasingly restless. They complained that too much power still remained in the hands of the magistrates and demanded a code of laws that would define and secure the rights of all. It was Rev. Nathaniel Ward of Ipswich who produced our next landmark of liberty. As the famous New England historian, John Palfrey, points out: "Ward was capable of the great business to which he was set...he announced the principal that life, liberty, or property was not to be invaded except by virtue of express law..." (CHOC, p. 261)

"The Body of Liberties...first lays down those fundamental principles relating to the sacredness of life, liberty, property, and reputation, which are the special subject-matter of a Bill of Rights. It then goes on to prescribe general rules of judicial proceedings to define the privileges and duties of freemen; to provide for justice to women, children, servants, and foreigners, and for gentle treatment of the brute creation...." (CHOC, p. 261, and see pp. 257-61 for extracts from the Body of Liberties)

This concept of a detailed enumeration of individual rights was to reappear in the first Ten Amendments of our Federal Constitution.

Self-Governing Quakers

Another colony which made important contributions to the development of Christian self-government in America was Pennsylvania established by Quaker William Penn. Although it was a proprietary colony – i.e., the Crown vested Penn with the right to govern it – he had no desire to be an autocratic ruler. On the contrary, he told the settlers that they were "at the mercy of no governor" and assured them, "you shall be governed by laws of your own making, and live a free and, if you will, a sober and industrious people." (CHOC, p. 265)

Penn believed that God had planted his colony and that He would "bless and make it the seed of a nation." Therefore, he was determined to "have a tender care to the government, that it will be well laid..." (CHOC, p. 265) Since he had been imprisoned in England in the Tower for heresy and again in Newgate Prison for defending the Quaker faith, he was deeply compassionate toward all victims of religious intolerance. (See CHOC, p. 262B for biographical details on Penn.)

The "Frame of Government" which Penn spent much time and thought in writing and which he signed on April 25, 1682 established religious liberty in Pennsylvania. *"All persons living in this province, who confess and acknowledge the One Almighty and Eternal God to be the Creator, Upholder, and Ruler of the world, and that hold themselves obliged in conscience to live peaceably and justly in civil society, shall in no wise be molested or prejudiced for their religious persuasion or practice, in matters of faith and worship; nor shall they be compelled at any time to frequent or maintain any religious worship, place or ministry whatsoever."* (T&L, p. 202)

This document vested the government in the governor and freemen through an elected provincial council and an assembly of all the freemen in the province. "Thus in this unusual colony – established through the faith and conviction of one man – God raised up the seed of righteous government – whose purpose was 'to make and establish such laws as shall best preserve true Christian and civil liberty, in opposition to all unchristian, licentious,

98

and unjust practices, whereby God may have his due, Caesar his due, and the people their due..."' (T&L, p. 203)

Standing Fast in Liberty

These outstanding Christian leaders – William Bradford, John Winthrop, Thomas Hooker, Roger Williams, Nathaniel Ward, and William Penn show what great things God can accomplish through self-governing Christians. By the efforts of these individuals and many others of diverse denominations, self-government was established in America. There is no limit to what we as self-governing Christians can accomplish today when we understand our history and "stand fast in the liberty wherewith Christ has made us free..." (Gal. 5:1)

We need to become active, self-governing Christians in our homes, our churches, our schools, and at all levels of our government. We need to participate in Christian civil government, by supporting capable, godly individuals who run for office and lending our own talents to this field if the Lord so leads us.

We need to take back the education of our children from the public schools which not only teach secular humanism but ignore our Christian history and even prohibit the Bible and prayer. As we re-learn the inspiring principles of our Christian history and teach them to our children in our homes and schools, we will be "repairers of the breach, the restorers of paths to dwell in," (Is. 58:12) and will ensure that our children will have – and be able to maintain – their precious heritage of liberty and self-government.

The following chart illustrates what God has done through self-governing individuals.

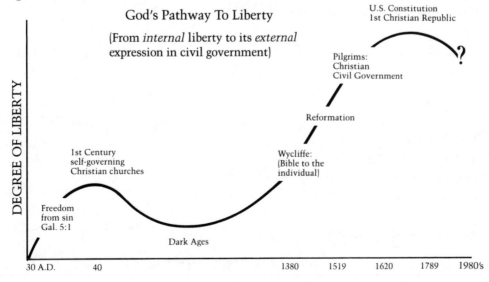

99

The Bible or the Bayonet

Liberty was won for us through the sacrifice of thousands of self-governing individuals over hundreds of years. Before we allow it to slip through our grasp, we should pause and consider the following words written by Robert C. Winthrop in 1852:

"Men, in a word, must necessarily be controlled either by a power within them, or by a power without them; either by the word of God, or by the strong arm of man, either by the Bible, or by the bayonet."[18]

Notes:

1. John Robinson, *The Works of John Robinson, Pastor of the Pilgrim Fathers*, ed., Robert Ashton, 3 vols. (London: John Snow, 1851), 2: 140-41.
2. Ibid., p. 141
3. Ibid.
4. Andrew C. McLaughlin, *Foundations of American Constitutionalism* (New York University, 1932: New York: Fawcett World Library, 1961), p. 17.
5. Leonard Bacon, *The Genesis of the New England Churches* (New York: Harper and Brothers, Publishers, 1874), p. 475.
6. Ibid., p. 477.
7. Brown, *The Pilgrim Fathers*, p. 255.
8. John Fiske, *The Beginnings of New England or The Puritan Theocracy in its Relation to Civil and Religious Liberty* (Boston and New York: Houghton, Mifflin and Company, 1900), p. 102.
9. Ibid.
10. H. Sheldon Smith, Robert T. Handy, Lefferts A. Loetscher, *American Christianity, An Historical Interpretation with Representative Documents*, Vol. 1: 1607-1820 (New York: Charles Scribner's Sons, 1960), pp. 100-101.
11. Ibid., p. 102
12. Brown, *Pilgrim Fathers*, p. 291.
13. Fiske, *Beginnings of New England*, p. 109.
14. Ibid., p. 124.
15. Ibid.
16. Peter Marshall and David Manuel, *The Light and the Glory* (Old Tappan, New Jersey: Fleming H. Revell Company, 1977), p. 207.

17. McLaughlin, *American Constitutionalism*, p. 34.
18. Hall, *Christian History of the American Revolution*, p. 20

Further Reading – Chapter 5

Chapter 5 – Study Questions

1. What kind of society do you have when external government is primary? And when internal Christian self-government is primary? _____
_____
_____

2. Why is a knowledge of the past important to preserve our liberty today? ___
_____
_____

3. What system of government did the Pilgrims discover in the New Testament? _____
_____

4. Was this system democratic or republican? _____
_____
_____

5. Did the element of monarchy enter into the New Testament church? In what way? _____
_____
_____

6. The Bishops of the Episcopal Church of England had monarchial powers. Why was this not in accord with the New Testament Church? _____
_____
_____

7. Who was monarch in the New Testament churches and the Pilgrim Church? _____
_____
_____

8. What effect did the Pilgrims have on the Puritans? _____
_____
_____

9. How does the material on the Puritans in this chapter refute the Puritan stereotype in many modern histories and media presentations? _____
_____
_____

10. What is a major pillar of American constitutionalism? _____
_____
_____

11. Why did the collective economic system in Plymouth fail? _____
_____
_____

12. Were the Christian ministers and laymen active in civil government in colonial days or did they leave it to others? _____
_____
_____ _____

13. As self-governing Christians, what is our duty in relation to civil government? _____
_____
_____

14. Why is it important for our children to learn the principles of Christian self-government as shown in our Christian history? _____
_____
_____

Chapter 6

Who Owns You and Your Property?

"And ye are not your own, For ye are bought with a price; therefore glorify God in your body, and in your Spirit, which are God's"

I Corinthians 6:20

DETAIL FROM THE SIGNING OF THE DECLARATION OF INDEPENDENCE
BY JOHN TRUMBULL

"Just as the Mayflower Compact united the Pilgrims in their shared Biblical vision of the body politic, so now the Declaration united a whole people in a solemn covenant."

Chapter 6

Who Owns You and Your Property?

There is perhaps no more important question to address at this critical hour of American history than "Who owns you and your property, God or Caesar?" If we do not settle this issue and settle it soon, what is left of our estates, our families, and our religious liberty will be confiscated by the humanist state.

Over the past 60 years, we, the American people, have been slowly boiled, so to speak, like an unwary frog, in a pan of candy-coated historical and theological distortions. Today we devote five months of every year to work as servants of the statist bureaucracy. That is how long it takes us to work off the tax burden at all levels. The Roman Empire fell with a tax burden of just over 20%, while we in America are facing well over a 40% tax burden.

The Question is: Who is God?

Many in our nation, when warned of the above facts, shrug their shoulders and say such things as, "that is the cost we must pay for our societal benefits" or "render unto Caesar the things that are Caesar's." They fail to recognize that whoever determines how you use your property will become your lord. The real question facing us today, is: "Who is sovereign?"

God, Satan, or Man?

A nation's, as well as an individual's, view of property and liberty will be determined by who it views as the ruler of this world. We have already seen in past chapters that the humanist, whether Greek, Roman, Russian or American, sees man and, more practically, the corporate man, "the state," as sovereign. Modern scholarship, the curriculum of most public schools, and the halls of Congress are dominated by this belief.

But how did this happen? In colonial America the God of the Bible was seen as sovereign over men and their property, reflecting the "Biblical world-view" of the Reformation. But in the past 100 years a disarming doctrine, which sees Satan as the sovereign of this world, has been accepted by many in Christian circles. Many Bible teachers today see Jesus as an absentee king who is concerned exclusively with building and maintaining His church until He returns to earth. They see Jesus as having the authority and right to rule, but as having given over powers to subjugate the world temporarily to Satan.

World-view of Many
20th Century Christians

World-view of the Reformation
and Early America

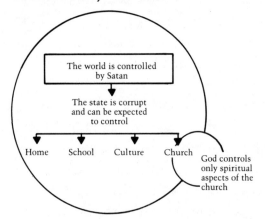

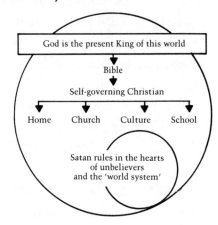

The world-view of the reformers was diametrically opposite to the view shown on the left. Jesus Christ is the ruler of the earth (I Tim. 6:16; Hebrews 2:14) and Satan, a defeated foe (John 12:3, Col. 2:15)

World View of the Secular Humanist

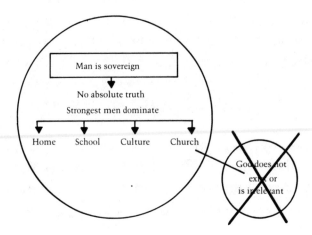

106

One's attitude toward the sovereignty issue is of paramount importance, because it affects what is done in every area of life. Here is the contrast:

If you see God ruling the earth:
1. Your commission is to subdue the earth and build godly nations through evangelizing and discipleship.
2. You see Christian culture as leavening all areas of life, replenishing the earth, and blessing all mankind.
3. All of God's world is His and every activity in life is a religious activity, to be seen as a spiritual work of God.
4. Reformation is expected if a nation is obedient to God's Word.

If you see Satan ruling the earth:
1. Your commission is just to concentrate on saving souls from this evil world.
2. You see Christian culture as a counter-culture, an isolated, persecuted minority in an evil world.
3. Church activity is primary and spiritual, while worldly pursuits are secular and to be dealt with only as a necessity.
4. Reformation is impossible since things must get worse because Satan is in control.

If you see man ruling the earth:
1. Your commission is whatever you choose to do with your life since man is autonomous.
2. You see Christian culture as old-fashioned, irrelevant and restrictive.
3. All human activity is guided by human reason and evolution. Man is just a higher animal in a mysterious universe.
4. Reformation is unnecessary and impossible since there are no absolute principles to which man should reform.

The above contrasts illustrate the importance of ideas in determining consequences, because to the degree Christians have abdicated their leadership role and denied the "crown rights of Jesus Christ," to that degree the humanists have filled the void.

Who Owned the Property of Our Forefathers?

In view of the foregoing, it is not surprising that the word "property" has a diminished value in today's dictionaries which define it superficially and in strictly materialistic terms. One dictionary defines it simply as "that which a person owns; the possession or possessions of a particular owner. Goods, land, etc...A piece of land or real estate." If this is our only sense of property, it is easy to be deluded by claims made by socialists and communists that "property rights" are separate from "human rights" and are far less important. Such an external view of property does not show its connection with the individual's life and liberty.

Dominion: The Foundation of Man's Property

This partial, purely external view of property, was not shared by our Bible-based Founding Fathers who fought the Revolutionary War in defense of their liberty and property.

Noah Webster's 1828 Dictionary sheds much more light on what the word property meant to our forefathers: "The exclusive right of possessing, enjoying and disposing of a thing; ownership. In the beginning of the world, the Creator gave to man dominion over the earth, over the fish of the sea and the fowls of the air, and over every living thing. This is the foundation of man's *property* in the earth and all its productions...The labor of inventing, making or producing any thing constitutes one of the highest titles to *property*...It is one of the greatest blessings of civil society that the *property* of citizens is well secured."

If the Pilgrims had been asked: "Who owns you and your property?" they would have answered in a word "God." Then they might have added: "We are free men who have been bought with a price – we are not slaves!" They recognized that they could not be any man's slave because they were God's property. "For ye are bought with a price; therefore glorify God in your body, and in your spirit which are God's." (1 Cor. 6:20) And, as Paul also said, "For we are his workmanship, created in Christ Jesus unto good works which God hath before ordained that we should walk in them." (Eph. 2:10)

Opposing Views of Property

If we consider the two parent colonies in their first years, we find that in Plymouth the Pilgrims strove to be self-supporting and, through Governor Bradford's wisdom in establishing private enterprise, they succeeded. They neither stole from the Indians nor demanded by the sword that the Indians barter their corn.

At Jamestown, on the other hand, the situation was different. As we have seen, many of the first settlers were hard-bitten soldiers of fortune or men on the run from English law who came to America in search of gold or other treasure. They were not interested in planting corn but preferred to barter with the Indians for their food – or to seize it by force.

Forced Labor and Low Productivity

While the tough, intrepid Captain John Smith was with them, he was often obliged to force them to work at the point of the sword. The colonists' unruly behavior demanded strong external government. After Smith returned to England, "everything tended fast to the wildest anarchy." Many colonists were

"so profligate, or desperate, that their country [England] was happy to throw them out as nuisances in society. Such persons were little capable of...the strict economy, and persevering industry, which their situation required." (CHOC, p. 160)

God's Providence Saves Colony

But, along with these unruly settlers, there was a strong, if small, nucleus of God-fearing, hard-working farmers and artisans – Virginia's future hope. When a terrible famine ensued, 500 settlers were reduced to 60 gaunt survivors in a mere six months. Just as they were abandoning Jamestown in a desperate attempt to reach Newfoundland, the hand of God intervened honoring the efforts of this faithful remnant. He had a plan for Virginia and would not have it abandoned.

"Before [Sir Thomas] Gates and the melancholy companions of his voyage had reached the mouth of the James River, they were met by Lord Delaware with three ships that brought a large recruit of provisions..." (CHOC, p. 161)

Evils of "The Common Ketell"

But the Virginia Colony's progress was still painfully slow. New settlers arrived with the same desire for quick gain and the same problems in productivity recurred. Because there were still those who preferred to get their supplies through plunder rather than productivity, a later governor, Sir Thomas Dale, finally invoked martial law in order to force production of the food they so desperately needed.

But, as in the case of the Plymouth Colony, the early settlers of Virginia were also fed "from the common Ketell" which, as at Plymouth, acted as a discouragement to those who were trying to work conscientiously, for the most idle and irresponsible were rewarded equally with the hard working and conscientious.

> *"...it was computed that the united industry of the colony, did not accomplish as much work in a week as might have been performed in a day, if each individual had laboured on his own account."* (CHOC, p. 162)

This is an interesting example of what happens when Karl Marx's dictum is actually in force: "From each according to his abilities, to each according to his needs."

Free Enterprise Brings Prosperity

The harsh, arbitrary rule that Dale meted out could not go on forever; it was self-defeating, because the moment it was relaxed, the same problems recurred. Finally, he divided part of the land into small plots and gave one to each individual as his property.

> *"From the moment that industry had the certain prospect of a recompense, it advanced with rapid progress."* (CHOC, p. 163)

Poor Stewards of God's Property

By 1619, a new type of colonist had begun to come to Virginia with plans to settle and work, and young women were sent from England to become their wives. But there were still many settlers who thought working by the sweat of their brow was beneath them, which may well account for the successful introduction of slavery into Virginia in 1619 when a Dutch ship from Guinea first brought a cargo of slaves to the planters.

Although slavery was condemned vigorously by the clergy in England and the colonies, it took root in the South, only to bring the ultimate national calamity foreseen by Virginia patriot George Mason in 1787. (See Chapter 7.)

It is important to understand that it was the Biblical idea of man as created by God which finally broke the bonds of slavery, first in England, through the tireless efforts of a minister and member of Parliament, Rev. William Wilberforce, and then later in America through the efforts of other godly men.

Many of the colonists who came to Jamestown in 1619, like those who came before, were intent on quick gain. Their new "gold" was tobacco, a crop they knew would sell at a high price. With total lack of foresight and self-control, they planted tobacco everywhere – even in the streets of Jamestown –

and neglected to raise adequate provisions of food. "...from eagerness for present gain, the planters disregarded every admonition." (CHOC, p. 163)

The result was that, pressed by lack of food, they began again "to renew their demands upon the Indians, who seeing no end of those exactions, their antipathy to the English name revived with additional rancor, and they began to form schemes of vengeance..." (CHOC, p. 163) These schemes later took effect in the Massacre of 1622 which almost wiped out the colony. But again God saved it from complete extermination through a Christian Indian's timely warning of the plot which helped save many lives.

The Representative System

In 1619, another event of great importance had taken place: A representative body, similar to the English House of Commons, was established, through the efforts of a Christian statesman, Sir Edwin Sandys, who was then Treasurer of the Virginia Company. The House of Burgesses, the first representative legislative body in America, was an important step in the direction of self-government for the colony (see CHOC, p. 165). By God's providence, this seed was to bear much fruit 100 years later when Virginia became the home of the nation's greatest statesmen.

Life, Liberty and Property

In the struggle for liberty that culminated in the Declaration of Independence, the individual's right to his property played a central role. In Boston, the Revolutionary battle cry was "Liberty and Property!" At the time of the Stamp Act in 1765, an organization called "The Sons of Liberty" was formed to resist the Act "by all lawful means." People marched through the streets of Boston to a gathering under an elm named the Liberty Tree, calling out, "Liberty, Property, and no Stamps!" (CHOC, p. 300)

Throughout the colonies, both in New England and the South, Life, Liberty, and Property were spoken of as a *single unit.* This was because John Locke, an English philosopher, had been inspired to present them in this way. The writings of "the great Mr. Locke" were widely read throughout the colonies. In his famous treatise, *Of Civil Government,* published in 1689, Locke speaks of men's "Lives, Liberties, and Estates, which I call by the general Name, Property." (CHOC, p. 91) He asserts that the "great and *Chief End* therefore, of Mens uniting into Commonwealths, and putting themselves under Government, *is the preservation of their Property."* (CHOC, p. 91)

111

"We Are His Workmanship"

Locke's Treatise closely examined property from the Biblical perspective. Echoing the words of the Apostle Paul, he wrote:

"For Men being all the Workmanship of one Omnipotent, and infinitely wise Maker: all the Servants of one Sovereign Master, sent into the World by his Order, and about his Business, they are his Property, whose Workmanship they are, made to last during his, not one anothers Pleasure..." (CHOC, p. 58)

Locke also refers to "those Grants God made of the World to Adam, and to Noah, and his Sons" which make it clear that God "has given the Earth to the Children of Men, given it to Mankind in common." (CHOC, pp. 63-64) If this is so, what about private property? Is such a concept unscriptural? Not at all! As Locke explains: "God, who hath given the World to Men in common, hath also given them reason to make use of it to the best Advantage of Life and Convenience." (CHOC, p. 64)

A Property in His Own Person

Then he makes a statement which was to strike a very responsive chord in the minds of America's colonial leaders of the Revolutionary period.

"Though the Earth and all inferior Creatures be common to all Men, yet every Man has a Property *in his own* Person: *This no Body has any right to but himself. The* Labour *of his Body, and the* Work *of his Hands, we may say, are properly his. Whatsoever then he removes out of the State that Nature hath provided, and left it in, he hath mixed his Labour with, and joyned to it something that is his own, and thereby makes it his Property."* (CHOC, p. 64)

Biblical Authority for Property

Because God did not intend the earth to remain "common and uncultivated," He gave it "to the use of the industrious and rational and Labour was to be his title to it..." (CHOC, pp. 65-66) God did not give the earth "to the Fancy or Covetousness of the Quarrelsome and Contentious," Locke added. Here is a reminder that the Tenth Commandment forbids us even to covet another person's property – the fruit of his labors. And, of course, "Thou shalt not steal" established the Biblical law regarding the individual's right to hold private property.

Conscience the Most Sacred Property

James Madison, who was to become known as "The Father of The Constitution," from early youth devoted himself to the study of history, particularly political history. He was familiar with all that had been written on the subject from the time of Aristotle. Like our other Founding Fathers, he was thoroughly familiar with the writings of John Locke and considered them ideal for educating youth in sound political principles. (See CHOC, p. 50A)

In an essay titled "Property," Madison gives a succinct and penetrating analysis of property from the Christian point of view:

"PROPERTY...In the former sense, a man's land, or merchandise, or money, is called his property. In the latter sense, a man has a property in his opinions and the free communication of them. He has a property of peculiar value in his religious opinions, and in the profession and practice dictated by them...He has an equal property in the free use of his faculties, and free choice of the objects on which to employ them. In a word, as a man is said to have a right to his property, he may be equally said to have a property in his rights...Government is instituted to protect property of every sort...Conscience is the most sacred of all property..." (CHOC. 248A)

Notice the disparity between what Locke and Madison saw as the purpose of government and what government has become. Today, rather than protecting our property, government expropriates it by punitive taxation.

Property: Internal and External

These views held by Locke and Madison show that they thought of property as being first of all *internal:*

— *Man has a property in his person*
— *Man has a property in the free use of his faculties*
— *Conscience is the most sacred of all property*

To these Christians, *external* property was something the individual produced from *within* by his abilities. And the quality of what he produced was also determined internally. "A good man out of the good treasure of the heart

113

bringeth forth good things: and an evil man out of the evil treasure bringeth forth evil things." (Matt. 12:35)

John Locke was a life-long member of the Church of England but one who advocated religious toleration. It was mainly to him that the great colonial political leaders in the South – mostly Church of England men – turned for clarification of their views on man's natural, God-given rights to "life, liberty and property." Such men as Madison, George Mason, and Patrick Henry were Christian leaders in the South who were thoroughly familiar with John Locke's writings. Thomas Jefferson, too, was greatly influenced by Locke although he did not share Locke's devout faith in Jesus Christ as Lord and Saviour. He did acknowledge the moral system of Jesus as the greatest the world had ever known.

Political Principles of the New England Clergy

In New England, too, Locke's writings were heavily quoted or paraphrased by political leaders like Samuel and John Adams. The clergy began quoting him in sermons as early as 1738. These ministers carefully taught their congregations the principles of Christian liberty. In the period between 1774-1776:

"Old and New Testament and classic writers...and often 'the great Mr. Locke' were cited [by the clergy] in proof of the duty as well as the right to resist tyranny and any attack upon the rights of men."[1]

Referring to liberty as man's Christian birthright, Rev. Gad Hitchcock, of Pembroke, Massachusetts said in a sermon in 1774, "Every man that is born into the world, as Mr. Locke, that prince of philosophers hath said, 'is born to it,' and every member of civil and religious society has an unalienable title to, and concern in it..."[2]

No Taxation Without Representation

Ever since the days of the Stamp Act in 1765, the colonists had been extremely vocal in their denial that the English Parliament had any right to tax their property without their consent. Although the Stamp Act was repealed, Great Britain continued to declare it had the right to tax the colonists. And after the repeal of the Townshend Acts taxing glass, lead, paper and tea, the British government issued an extraordinary series of Royal Instructions that "required the dissolution of assemblies...negatived arbitrarily the choice of speakers; provided for the maintenance of local officers; and thus entirely ignored the local legislation for the support of government..." (CHOC, p. 317)

Arbitrary Law Supplants Local Self-Government

This attempt to supplant local self-government with totally arbitrary rule, aroused great indignation throughout the colonies. The colonial leaders kept stressing the dangers to liberty if they consented to being governed by these tyrannical Royal Instructions.

"Among these leaders Samuel Adams was pre-eminent. He had been steadily rising in reputation in Massachusetts and abroad...He gave to the cause the whole of his time...masterly state papers attest his intelligence, industry and influence." (CHOC, p. 318)

A devout Christian of the highest character, Samuel Adams sacrificed much for the cause of liberty. Historian George Bancroft describes him as a "statesman of a clear and logical mind...His will resembled well-tempered steel, which may ply, but will not break." (T&L, pp. 251-252) His untiring efforts on behalf of the cause of liberty in the colonies – he was among the first to see the need for independence from the Mother Country – earned him the title "Father of the Revolution." In 1772, Samuel Adams produced one of America's great state papers:

"The Rights of the Colonists as Men, as Christians, and as Subjects"

1772

There is a strong resemblance between this document and the Declaration of Rights of the First Continental Congress in 1774, and the great Declaration of Independence of 1776. The document's first terse sentence under the heading of "Rights of the Colonists as Men" is: "Among the Natural rights of the Colonists are these: First, a right to life; Secondly, to liberty; Thirdly, to property; together with the right to support and defend them in the best manner they can." (CHOC, p. 365)

Because Adams saw liberty as the gift of God, he said that man could not "voluntarily become a slave."

"In short, it is the greatest absurdity to suppose it in the power of one, or any number of men, at the entering into society, to renounce their essential

natural rights, or the means of preserving those rights; when the grand end of civil government...is for the support, protection, and defence of those very rights; the principal of which...are Life, Liberty, and Property." (CHOC, p. 367).

In the center-piece of his paper, The Rights of The Colonists as Christians, he says, *"These may be best understood by reading and carefully studying the institutes of the great Law Giver and Head of the Christian Church, which are to be found clearly written and promulgated in the New Testament."*

In the section, "Rights of The Colonists as Subjects," Adams maintains that the legislative branch of government "has no right to absolute, arbitrary power over the lives and fortunes of the people; nor can mortals assume a prerogative not only too high for men, but for angels, and therefore reserved for the exercise of the Deity alone." (CHOC, p. 368) Nor can the legislative rule by "extemporary arbitrary decrees." On the contrary, the rights of subjects are to be decided by "standing and known laws."

When he comes to discuss property specifically, he asserts that "the supreme power cannot justly take from any man any part of his property, without his consent in person or by his representative." And he challenges the right of the English House of Commons "at pleasure to give and grant the property of the Colonists."

The first sentence of the next paragraph must have had an electrifying effect when it was read at town meetings or by colonial firesides. Those who knew Adams could fairly hear the righteous wrath in his voice thundering like that of a Biblical Samuel: "Now what liberty can there be when property is taken away without consent?" Here he touched the vital connection between the individual's property and his liberty. For his property not only sustains his life, but is the bulwark of his liberty and his ability to support God's work. If it can be taken away from him without his consent then he has lost his liberty.

Starved into Submission

Many today in totalitarian countries have learned that you cannot lose political liberty without also losing economic liberty. In the Soviet Union those who stand up against the state in accord with their conscience, "the most sacred of all property," are often prohibited from working and are thus literally starved to death or into submission (See *Under The Rubble* by Alexander Solzhenitsyn.)

Momentum of Events

After the Boston Tea Party in December 1773, Great Britain resolved to punish Massachusetts by blockading the Port of Boston and abolishing local self-government. But, instead of intimidating the other colonies, these acts only united them behind Massachusetts. Virginia called for the First Continental Congress which convened at Philadelphia on September 5, 1774 and drew up a Declaration of Resolves and Grievances. Now events gathered momentum. English statesmen Pitt and Burke counseled moderation in dealing with the colonies, but neither Parliament as a whole nor the King was in the mood to redress the grievances of the colonists.

One of the delegates to the first Continental Congress was Patrick Henry who urged that the colonies unite in their opposition to Great Britain, forgetting distinctions between Virginians, Pennsylvanians, and New Englanders in their determination to stand for their God-given rights to their life, liberty and property. Henry's love of liberty had been well-nurtured from his childhood when his mother took him week after week to hear the great Presbyterian minister, Dr. Samuel Davies, a staunch defender of religious and political liberty and an eloquent preacher. Young Henry absorbed not only something of Davies' oratorical style, but also his ideas of religious liberty, and his early career as a lawyer was notable for his defense of Baptist ministers and other religious dissenters from persecution by the state-supported Episcopal Church in Virginia.

Liberty or Death

Upon adjournment of the Continental Congress in October 1774, Henry returned to Virginia. Here, on March 20, 1775, he made his most famous speech before the Virginia Convention assembled at Richmond in St. John's Episcopal Church. Henry was convinced that reconciliation with England was no longer possible – and events at Lexington and Concord were soon to prove him right.

Henry proposed resolutions putting Virginia into an active military defence posture, but others at the Convention opposed him. Finally, in his great speech that turned the tide in favor of Independence, he delivered a series of searching questions, followed by the only possible answer:

"What...has there been in the conduct of the British ministry for the last ten years to justify hope? Are fleets and armies necessary to a work of love and reconciliation? These are implements of subjugation...And what have we to oppose to them? Shall we try argument? We have been trying that for the last ten years...In vain may we indulge the fond hope of reconciliation...An appeal to arms and to the God of Hosts is all that is left us!...Three millions of people, armed in the holy cause of liberty...are invincible...We shall not fight alone. A just God presides over the destinies of nations...Is life so dear, or peace so sweet, as to be purchased at the price of chains and slavery? Forbid it, Almighty God! — I know not what course others may take; but as for me, give me liberty, or give me death." (CHOC, p. 346A)

The Shot Heard Around the World

On April 18, 1775, General Gage, the military governor sent out from England to subdue the rebellious colony of Massachusetts, secretly planned a raid on the patriots' ammunition stores at Concord. He also hoped to arrest Samuel Adams and John Hancock who were rumored to be in nearby Lexington. Providentially, patriot Dr. Joseph Warren got wind of the plot and sent Paul Revere and William Dawes through the countryside that night sounding the alarm. Revere arrived at the home of Rev. Jonas Clark, where Adams and Hancock were staying, just in time to warn them to make their escape.

Rev. Clark was one of New England's great patriot pastors. For years, he had been preaching on the basic Biblical principles undergirding righteous government: that the people's rights to their life, liberty and property came from God; that the people had the right to form their governments by sacred covenant before God.

"The town records of Lexington contain many important documents which discussed the great questions involved in the national struggle for Independence. In 1765, the citizens vindicated the popular movement in respect to the Stamp Act....In 1768, they argued...against the right of Great Britain to tax America. In 1772, they resolved...to seek redress for daily increasing wrongs; and in 1774, they took measures to supply themselves with ammunition, arms and other requisites for military defence. What hero drew those masterly papers, defended their principles, and fired the people at all hazards to defend them? History

has recorded the fact, the Reverend Jonas Clark was their author and chief defence." (T&L, p. 49)

On April 19, 1775, the British detachment of soldiers arrived at Lexington Green to find the town's militia assembled and ready to defend their community. The British officer ordered the militia to disperse. According to Rev. Clark, who saw all that happened that day from his church on the Green, the British began to fire on the militia even as it was dispersing. Only then did the men of Lexington return the enemy's fire. Eight of them were killed.

This conduct is in character with their pastor's teaching that only a defensive war could be just. The Battle of Lexington, brief as it was, gave the patriots at Concord the time they needed to collect their arms and ammunition and hide them carefully as well as to muster their militia. These arms were their property, obtained to ensure their means of defence and should not be taken by the British for use against them. They would die first! Here, too, at Concord, the patriots were not the first to fire. Frothingham relates that the British posted a guard of a hundred men at the Old North Bridge.

"About ten o'clock, as a body of militia were approaching this bridge, the guard fired upon them, when more citizens were killed and wounded." (CHOC, p. 346)

The Minute Men defended themselves well. They forced the British into a disorderly retreat. By the time the British reached Charlestown, they were on the run and only narrowly missed being defeated by 700 militia bearing down on them just as they reached the shelter of the British fleet. On that day, the British lost 273 men, the American militiamen, 93. But if the Lexington farmers had not made their stand – thus buying time for Concord – if Revere had not reached Hancock and Adams in time to warn them...In short, if Providence had not intervened several times, the day would have been a total disaster for the Americans.

Connecticut's Day of Prayer

One thing the people of Lexington probably did not realize was that on that very day, the Colony of Connecticut held a day of prayer and fasting for all the colonies. When Governor Trumbull proclaimed April 19, 1775 as the date, he little dreamed what momentous events would be taking place at Lexington! His proclamation asked:

> *"...that God would graciously pour out his Holy Spirit on us to bring us to a thorough Repentance and effectual Reformation that our iniquities may not be our ruin: that He would restore, preserve and secure the Liberties of this and all the other British American colonies, and make the Land a mountain of Holiness, and Habitation of Righteousness forever."*[3]

Reconciliation or Revolution?

When the Congress reconvened on May 10, 1775, the war with the Mother Country had begun. Still, some members of Congress hoped for a reconciliation – despite Lexington and Concord. Congress drew up another petition and sent it to England hoping against hope that the King would listen to their plea for redress of grievances. Instead the British monarch cut off all trade with the colonies and declared them to be in rebellion. Now many colonial leaders began to see that independence must be declared.

The Virginia Declaration of Rights

But it was not until a year later, on May 14, 1776, that Virginia took the step of convening its House of Burgesses as a free convention of delegates – the royal governor having fled – and voted for independence. George Mason was then asked to draw up a Declaration of Rights which was to have a two-fold importance: first, it was used subsequently by many of the colonies as the basis of their declarations; second, it was undoubtedly one of the documents that influenced Thomas Jefferson as he wrote the Declaration of Independence.

On June 12, 1776 the Convention approved Mason's great declaration which states in Section 1: *"That all men are by nature equally free and independent, and have certain inherent rights, of which, when they enter into a state of society, they cannot, by any compact, deprive or divest their posterity, namely the enjoyment of life and liberty, with the means of acquiring and possessing property, and pursuing and obtaining happiness and safety.*[4]

Here is an acknowledgment of the sacredness of natural rights which men have no moral authority to relinquish, because they come from God. No decision by any majority could be valid against these God-given rights.

Historian Richard Frothingham says of the Declaration of Independence, *"It includes far more than it expresses; for by recognizing human equality and brotherhood, and the individual as the unit of society, it accepts the Christian idea of man as the basis of political institutions..."* (CHOC, p. 359) Daniel Elazar, a distinguished contemporary scholar, refers to the Declaration as "the founding covenant of the American people." Such scholars as Elazar and Andrew C. McLaughlin recognize the covenant roots of our nation. Just as the Mayflower Compact united the Pilgrims in their shared Biblical vision of the body politic, so now the Declaration united a whole people in a solemn covenant.

It is true that Thomas Jefferson's draft of the Declaration included only a reference to "nature's God" but when it was thrashed out in committee by John Adams, Robert Livingston, Benjamin Franklin and Roger Sherman, they added the important words, "they are endowed by their Creator with certain unalienable rights." Then, when the Declaration was debated on the floor of Congress, the phrase "appealing to the Supreme Judge of the World, for the rectitude of our intentions" was added, as were the eloquent words "with a firm reliance on the protection of divine Providence." This brought the Declaration into complete harmony with the Christian consensus of Congress.[5]

The Pursuit of Happiness

But why did Congress allow Jefferson to change the commonly used phrase "Life, liberty and property" to "Life, liberty and the pursuit of happiness"? Did not this weaken their stated resolve to defend their rights?

It is true that the Resolution adopted by Congress in 1774 stated simply that the colonists had a right to "life, liberty, and property." But the use of the word "happiness" by Jefferson (and also by Mason in his Declaration of Rights) was not considered as a curtailment of the idea of property, but, rather, as an enlargement of it. A popular treatise on the Principles of Natural Law had been written by a Swiss writer, Jean Jacques Burlemaqui, in 1774 in which the author used this phraseology. Certainly, the Founders knew that the right to property – internal or external – was vital to ensure happiness.

John Dickinson wrote in his "Letters From A Pennsylvania Farmer" that:

> "...we cannot be happy, without being free – that we cannot be free, without being secure in our property – that we cannot be secure in our property, if without our consent, others may, as by right, take it away..."[6]

His words take us right back to the individual's right to the fruits of his own labors which he has been commanded by God to perform. Both the Declaration of Rights and the Declaration of Independence stand as examples of the Christian idea of man and government. Rosalie Slater reminds us:

> "...as the words of the Declaration of Independence resound down the years, we can remember that 'the price of liberty is eternal vigilance.' Because the American Revolution is a Christian revolution for individual freedom – or salvation – it is never over." (T&L, p. 254)

Sacrifices of the Founding Fathers

It is humbling to consider the great price the Founding Fathers were willing to pay to secure the rights we enjoy today. Our Founders were willing to sacrifice their lives, liberty and estates in order to preserve these rights for their posterity. Of the 56 signers of the Declaration, 9 died in the war; 5 were captured and suffered severely at the hands of the British; the homes of 12 were either burned to the ground, looted, or defaced by occupying troops.

Thomas Nelson, Jr.

A planter from Yorktown, Nelson succeeded Thomas Jefferson as governor of Virginia, put up his own property as collateral and raised almost two million dollars to help the new nation fight the War of Independence. When the notes came due, he was unable to pay and lost those properties. At the final battle of Yorktown, Nelson personally directed the cannon fire that destroyed his own home which had been appropriated by the British as field headquarters for General Cornwallis.

Robert Morris

Known to historians as "the Financier of the American Revolution," Morris became a strong patriot as early as the days of the Stamp Act crisis in 1765. As a prosperous Philadelphia merchant, he patriotically supported the non-importation agreement (by which the colonies refused to import any more British goods until their grievances were redressed) even though he knew this would mean significant financial losses for his business. In November 1775, the Pennsylvania Legislature chose him as a delegate to the Continental Congress where he was put to work to provide naval armaments. This was the beginning of many outstanding services to the Congress and the people of the United States.

Crucial Contributions to the Success of the War

So great was his conviction that the war must be won, that when the Continental Army was experiencing serious reverses at the end of 1776 and had just been forced to retreat across New Jersey, Morris raised ten thousand dollars upon his personal credit. Without his help at this crucial moment, historians point out that Washington would not have been able to hold his starving troops together or to recross the Delaware and win a much-needed victory at the Battle of Trenton.

In 1781, Congress appointed Morris General Financial Agent of the United States (i.e., Secretary of the Treasury). He had such a high reputation as a businessman that he was able to raise tens of thousands of dollars at a time when Congress could not even raise a thousand. But more greatly to his honor is the fact that, according to official records, the great campaign of 1781 at Yorktown, which virtually won the war, could not have taken place without the aid of Robert Morris. This conclusive campaign was waged solely on his financial credit! Robert Morris unhesitatingly risked his property and his reputation in order to secure the rights of all his fellow Americans. Never let it be said that one man can do nothing significant to turn the tide of history![7]

George Washington

But perhaps the greatest sacrifices were made by George Washington. On his own insistence, he served throughout the war without salary and sacrificed the years he so much wanted to spend as a farmer on his estate at Mount Vernon. He felt called by Divine Providence to serve his country for the better part of 45 years. It was only at the age of 66 that he was finally able to retire to the peace of Mount Vernon. Within three years he was dead. Yet, he would not begrudge all that he sacrificed if he knew that we *valued* the liberty which he and so many other patriots, whose names we will never know, fought to achieve. He, like so many others, gave up the life he loved in order to ensure the liberty we now enjoy.

Christian Social Financing

Do we contemporary Christians need to make sacrifices of *our* time and money in order to solve today's many pressing social and economic problems? Or should we be content to relinquish control over the fruits of our labor to an all-powerful state and allow it to become the provider of the poor? Or do we perhaps desire to hold onto all we have earned and give only token amounts to help those in need? Is there an alternative to either self-centered laissez-faire or to the welfare state? Yes, there is! We must confess that as government spending at every level is curtailed, taxes are reduced, and budgets balanced – as they should be – the needs of the poor, the handicapped, and the aged will become more pressing.

Edward A. Powell and Rousas John Rushdoony, in their book *Tithing and Dominion*, come to grips with all these questions. They acknowledge that an advanced nation, such as ours, cannot exist without "a vast network of social institutions which require financing and support."[8] But, it is because of the failure of American Christians that such financing is not forthcoming from the private sector. "If a Christian concept of social financing is lacking, then the state moves in quickly to supply the lack and gain the social control which results."[9]

This is exactly what has happened through our falling away from the Bible's commands. For, as these authors point out, the Bible provides the tithe as the foundational law for society. Furthermore, in Biblical law there is no such thing as a property tax. (After all, the earth belonged to God; it was not for man to tax it!) The immunity of land from taxation by the state meant liberty. A man could not be dispossessed of his land; every man had a basic security in his property."[10]

A Tale of Two Cities

In the early days of our nation, the tithe supported not only churches, but church schools and colleges, and provided for a variety of other social needs. In Rushdoony's "Revolt Against Maturity" he discusses how one New England town coped with radical population changes wholly by the use of the tithe. Salem, Massachusetts, saw a population boom between 1795 and 1845, doubling its population several times over until it had grown from a village into a city. There was a flood of foreign immigrants and one would think that the town's character would have been completely changed and that the burden of such an influx of people would have caused a complete dislocation of its social fabric. But, as a matter of fact, the needs of the immigrants — as well as of the town's own citizens — were met through a variety of tithing agencies that cared for the poor, provided education, job-training, children's education, Bible courses, and taught the immigrants English. Salem is just one example of our nation when it was still actively obedient to God's Scriptural laws. Salem shows what conscientious tithing Christians can accomplish in the field of social welfare. As Powell and Rushdoony point out: "Conscientious and intelligently administered tithing by even a small minority can do much to reconstruct a land."[11]

Compare this with the situation in Miami, Florida, today where the influx of Haitian refugees has caused a crisis for the entire state with riots, burnings, and a high crime rate. Only Christian love expressed through voluntary tithing associations can solve this problem. Charity means love, and only individuals, not government agencies, can give love.

Our Responsibility as God's Stewards

We must act upon our knowledge of God's principles of property, stewardship, and economy, giving to the world a positive example of the benefit of obeying God's principles. If we desire a cut-back in services and control by the Federal Government and more local autonomy, as our President has called for, then we ourselves must be weaned from the government dole. We must also influence our families and our churches to be self-governing. If we are going to cut back on government services and welfare, then we must honestly begin to tithe so that the real personal and social needs of society can be met through the private sector (see Chapter 8).

We must stop our own deficit spending and obey the Biblical admonition to be debt-free and live within our means ("owe no man anything, but to love one another," Romans 13:8). We must also guard our motives so that our desire to preserve private property is not just a desire for selfish gain, but that it is truly a desire to preserve the sovereignty of God and the stewardship over all that God has given us to do.

If we refuse to do these things, and other actions that our principles will dictate, then we have very little hope or right to expect a restoration of our liberty. But if we obey our Lord, we have every hope and promise of success (Joshua 1:8, 9). Our economic and political future rests not in the hands of foreign powers or governmental bureaucrats in our own land, but in our own hands through our obedience to God.

We must once again lead our nation, through our example, into the art of self-government and proper stewardship of God's property.

NOTES:

1. Alice M. Baldwin, *The New England Clergy and The American Revolution* (New York: Frederick Ungar Publishing Co., 1958), p. 129.
2. Hall, *Christian History of The American Revolution*, p. 41.
3. Ibid., p. 407.
4. McLaughlin, *Foundations of American Constitutionalism*, p. 78.
5. Frank Donovan, *Mr. Jefferson's Declaration* (New York: Dodd, Mead, & Co., 1968), p. 96.
6. Hall, *Christian Self-Government with Union*, p. 445
7. See Benjamin Lossing, *Signers of The Declaration* (New York: J. C. Derby Publisher, 1856). See also the article on Morris in the Spring Issue of *The Restoration Press,* published by Restore America Institute, P. O. Box 23343, Columbus, Ohio 43223.
8. Edward A Powell and Rousas John Rushdoony, *Tithing and Dominion* (Vallecito, California: Ross House Books, 1979), p. 1.
9. Ibid.
10. Ibid., p. 4.
11. Ibid.

Further Reading – Chapter 6

Chapter 6 – Study Questions

1. What do human rights include and who grants them? _____
_____

2. Who owns us and to whom are we accountable for our property? _____
_____

3. What is the Biblical authority for the individual's right to property? _____
_____

4. What property does every person in the world possess? _____
_____

5. Why does no one but you have the right to the fruits of your labor? _____
_____

6. Our Founding Fathers thought of property as internal and external. Give some examples of internal property. _____
_____

7. What is external property? Give some examples. _____
_____

8. What is the most sacred of all property? _____
_____

9. Was collective ownership of property part of God's intention for man? _
_____

10. What is morally wrong about the Marxist system that takes from each according to his abilities and gives to each according to his needs? _____

_____

11. Shouldn't the government tax the affluent in order to provide for the needy? _____

_____

12. If not, who should provide for the needy and how should it be done? __

_____

13. What were the three elements of a man's property discussed by John Locke and the Founding Fathers? _____

_____

14. What happens to religious and civil liberties when you lose economic liberty, i.e., the right to your property? _____

_____

15. Why are most Christians today not active politically in defending their property rights? _____

_____

16. The Declaration of Independence speaks of men's rights to life, liberty and the pursuit of happiness. What did the founding Fathers feel was necessarily included in happiness? _____

_____

Chapter 7

The Genius of
the American Republic

"For unto us a child is born, unto us a son is given: and the government shall be upon his shoulder...of the increase of his government and peace there shall be no end"

Isaiah 9:6,7

SIGNING OF THE CONSTITUTION
BY HOWARD CHANDLER CHRISTY

"Just as the heart of the covenant of ancient Israel consists of two parts, the Decalogue or Ten Commandments with its electrifying statement of fundamental principles and the Book of the Covenant with its more detailed framework of basic laws of the Israelite Commonwealth, so too does that of the American covenant consist of two basic documents serving the same purposes – the Declaration of Independence and the Constitution."

– Daniel J. Elazar
(See Foreword)

Chapter 7

The Genius of the American Republic

How can America be a Christian republic when, under our Constitution, there is supposedly a separation of church and state? To answer this question it is necessary to understand what our Founding Fathers were trying to accomplish. They were intent upon preventing any one denomination from imposing its views on the self-governing individual through the power of civil government. They viewed conscience as the most sacred of all property to be carefully protected by the government. When they said in the First Amendment to the Constitution: "Congress shall make no law respecting an establishment of religion, or prohibiting the free exercise thereof...", they were making it clear that they would not live under a national state church or establishment which could demand their membership and financial support. It was the tyranny of religious conformity that they opposed. But to say that they intended a secular state in which religion would play no part is to fly in the face of all evidence to the contrary. They never envisioned a secular state where God's moral laws would be systematically and deliberately flouted. Yet this has come to pass. (See Question 6, Chapter 1.)

The Spirit and the Letter

Our State governments and the Federal government were built largely upon principles which the Founders derived from their study of the Scriptures. The form of our republic still remains, but the spirit – which is Christianity – has been stifled. Without this animating spirit, the letter is dead. (II Cor. 3:6)

"To understand the American Christian Constitution as the Christian form of government, it is necessary to consider its two spheres – the spirit *and the* letter *— the* internal *and the* external. *Both spheres must be active in order that the Constitution function to preserve the basic republican spirit of individual liberty. Today we still have the* letter *of the Constitution. That is, we still go through most of the legal processes of the* structure *of the Constitution in enacting legislation, and in the executive and judicial branches. But the* spirit *which was intended and understood by our Founding Fathers is missing – and has been for the last one hundred years. That* spirit *was the Christian foundation of our Constitution – the Faith of our Fathers – and as our nation has fallen away from its foundations – the essence of that faith – our Constitution has become a hollow shell."* (T&L, p. 240)

As Americans have forgotten the Biblical foundation of their government, they have allowed a subtle transformation of the doctrine of separation of *church* and state into separation of *religion* and state, so that now Christianity can no longer receive a hearing in the schools; prayer and Bible reading are prohibited; laws legalizing abortion are passed and upheld by the judiciary; the rights of Christian pastors to express their convictions on governmental matters in the pulpit – as our Colonial pastors did – are curtailed and penalized in an attempt to prevent all meaningful criticism of the secular state.

Because our form of government is derived in all its parts from Biblical principles, it cannot be understood without comprehending those principles, nor can it be made to work as our Founding Fathers intended. Our failure to grasp their intentions may be seen in the following contrasts:

OUR FOUNDING FATHERS ESTABLISHED:	TODAY WE HAVE:
1. Republican government representing *each individual's* rights.	1. A majoritarian democracy representing the will of the majority – even when it tramples on the rights of the individual.

132

2. Separation of powers – legislative, executive and judicial – in order to protect the individual against the tyranny resulting from concentration of power.

   A. A legislative power to respect the individual's rights to his own life, liberty and property and to his Christian self-government.

   B. Specifically limited powers for the presidency.

   C. The Supreme Court as the interpreter of law in accord with the Constitution which is undergirded by Biblical law.

3. A dual system of government: a) the states retaining most powers; b) the Federal Government having only those powers necessary for its sphere of authority.

2. Balance of powers upset by a) increasing predominance of the presidency; b) the Supreme Court usurping the rights of the legislative branch; c) the most important branch, the representative, greatly weakened.

   A. A legislative branch that passes laws encroaching upon the individual's right of self-government and his rights to his own life, liberty and property.

   B. Presidential powers frequently bypassing Congress through "executive orders."

   C. The Supreme Court flouting Biblical law in many of its rulings and often usurping the rights of the legislative branch.

3. A strong unitary government with powers being absorbed by Washington, the states steadily losing their local self-government and sources of revenue to the Federal Government.

This decline would never have come to pass if the American Christian had not stepped aside from the political arena and retreated into purely personal religion leaving the field of civil government largely to the secular humanists. Of course, if we had known the distinctively Christian nature of the elements of our government, we would not have turned our backs on our heritage.

The Biblical Perspective of Our Founders

What is it that identifies America as a Christian nation? What are the elements of our form of government that are distinctively Biblical? These are questions that every American should be able to answer. Contrary to common belief today, most of our Founders were Christians and, in contrast to the average person today, they understood that *every* nation has a theological and philosophical basis. Were they here today, they would not find it difficult to understand that even atheistic Marxist cultures, such as those that increasingly prevail around the globe, are religious to the core – preaching by force the doctrine of man as the measure of all things. In their time, our Founders had the example of the French revolutionaries who were preaching much the same thing. But our Founding Fathers, with few exceptions, were diametrically opposed to the atheistic path chosen by the French revolutionaries.

Even though this is so, it is important to remember that our nation was established as a Christian nation, not because all the Founders or all the people were Christian, but because it was founded on the Christian view of man and government that prevailed at that time. Those who try to dismiss the historical evidence that ours is a Christian republic often point to two or three unbelieving Founding Fathers as if they were representative of all the rest. But the contrary is true, and these few individuals had to bow before the prevailing Christian perspective that surrounded them. The main elements of our government sprang from this perspective.

The First Pillar of the Constitution:
The Principle of Representation

One of the fundamental elements of our new political system was a new phenomenon in the world: the American representive system of government which may justly be called the first pillar of the Constitution. In 1783, the Rev. Dr. Ezra Stiles, then President of Yale University, said in a sermon:

All the forms of civil polity have been tried by mankind, except one, and that seems to have been reserved in Providence to be realized in America..." [That wonder was a unique kind of republic] "...a democratical polity for millions, standing upon the broad basis of the people at large, amply charged with property..." (CHOC, p. 382)

134

Setting the Stage

But first the stage had to be set. As we have seen in Chapter 3, the Bible had to be put into the hands of individuals. This gave them not only the *desire* for liberty, but the *ability* to be self-governing which, in turn, safeguards liberty. Second, a land had to be provided that was separated from Old World despotism of monarchs and separated, too, from the religious skepticism which was to arise during the so-called Enlightenment. Third, a people had to be prepared who shared a Biblical world view of the nature of man and government. The Biblical view of man drove them to develop a form of government that would neither depend blindly upon the will of the masses nor give absolute power to one man. They knew that, as Lord Acton succinctly stated, "Power corrupts and absolute power corrupts absolutely."

The Sin Nature of Man

Why did they understand the corrupting nature of power so well? Because they shared the Biblical view of the sin nature of man. Therefore, they could not share the view of the French philosopher, Jean Jacques Rousseau, that man is naturally good and able to perfect himself. Nor could they share his enthusiasm for the "general will." The general will could be dead wrong; it could trample on the God-given rights of the individual. But neither did they believe what King George had tried to tell them: that they must bow to the decrees of the sovereign as a leader by divine right.

A Balanced, Biblical Outlook

The balanced, Biblical outlook of our Founding Fathers is exemplified in both the Old and New Testament and produced a new view of the body politic beginning with representative government. For example, Moses was exhorted by his father-in-law, Jethro, to choose qualified judges or representatives to help him guide and direct Israel. (Exod. 18:13-21) The New Testament churches were admonished to choose elders and deacons (representatives) based upon the qualifications laid out in I Tim. 3 and Titus 1:6-9. Because they understood the Biblical view of government, the American republics and the great Federal republic they created were quite different from all the republics that had preceded them.

Defining a Republic

What then is a republic? The word is from the Latin and means simply "public affairs." Noah Webster, in his 1828 Dictionary, defines it as "A

135

Commonwealth; a state in which the exercise of the sovereign power is lodged in representatives elected by the people. In modern usage, it differs from a democracy or democratic state, in which the people exercise the powers of sovereignty in person. Yet the democracies of Greece are often called *republics.*" Let us survey the nature of these so-called republics, comparing them with the American model.

Tyrannical Greek Democracies

These Greek democracies were turbulent, easily swayed assemblies of the whole people, who came under the influence of silver-tongued orators. Hannah More writes of the Athenians:

> *This unsettled government, which left the country perpetually exposed to the tyranny of the few, and the turbulence of the many, was never bound together by any principle of union, by any bond of interest, common to the whole community...The restraint of laws was feeble; the laws themselves were often contradictory; often ill administered..."* *(T&L, p. 161)*

James Madison, known as "the Father of the Constitution," thoroughly studied both Greek and Roman history and understood government from the Christian perspective having studied theology and ethics under the Rev. Dr. John Witherspoon at the College of New Jersey. Dr. Witherspoon prepared Madison and many other young men for distinguished public careers. As a signer of the Declaration of Independence, Witherspoon was heart and soul with the patriot cause and served as a delegate to the Continental Congress for seven years. From him, James Madison imbibed the Christian view of man as a sinner who could not be trusted with unlimited power. Sharing this view of life, as did most of the Founding Fathers, Madison saw the dangers of unrestrained majority rule remarking that a society made up of those

> *"who assemble and administer the government in person, can admit of no cure for the mischiefs of faction. A common passion or interest will, in almost every case, be felt by a majority of the whole...and there is nothing to check the inducements to sacrifice the weaker party or an obnoxious individual. Hence it is that such democracies have ever been spectacles of turbulence and contention; have ever been found incompatible with personal security and the rights of property; and have in general been as short in their lives as they have been violent in their deaths."*[1]

Defect of the Roman Republic

But if the Greek democracies did not hold the key to political wisdom, what about the great Roman republic? Historian John Fiske saw that Rome had been unable to protect personal liberty because of a fundamental defect:

"Now if we ask why the Roman government found itself thus obliged to sacrifice personal liberty and local independence to the paramount necessity of holding the empire together, the answer will point us to the essential and fundamental vice of the Roman method of nation-making. It lacked the principle of representation...Its senates were assemblies of notables...There was no notion of such a thing as political power delegated by the people to representatives who were to wield it away from home and out of sight of their constituents...When, therefore, the Roman popular government...had come to extend itself over a large part of the world, it lacked the one institution by means of which government could be carried on over so vast an area without degenerating into despotism..." (CHOC, p. 13)

When Caesar Augustus seized the reins of power, this is exactly what happened. In his study of the ancient republics, Madison saw that a truly representative principle would solve this very problem because it acted

"to refine and enlarge the public views, by passing them through the medium of a chosen body of citizens, whose wisdom may best discern the true interest of their country, and whose patriotism and love of justice will be least likely to sacrifice it to temporary or partial considerations."[2]

While Madison hoped that the men chosen to office would be godly men who would act from the highest motives, he was under no illusion as to the sin nature of man. He knew that unless their powers were limited

"Men of factious tempers, of local prejudices, or of sinister designs, may, by intrigue, by corruption, or by other means, first obtain the suffrages, and then betray the interests, of the people."[3]

Madison's Political Presuppositions

Throughout his career, Madison was always acutely aware of "the mischiefs of faction" which he was convinced could only by handled effectively through a separation of powers. His college mentor, Dr. Witherspoon, had long held this view. Indeed, in order to understand Madison's political principles, it is necessary to understand his theological roots. As scholar James H. Smylie writes: "Madison's theological orientation is of paramount importance."[4] Why? Because, as Smylie notes, "the source of his political presuppositions" lies in the Calvinism he imbibed from Witherspoon during his formative years. While Madison was to come under many influences throughout his life, it was Witherspoon's which was of critical importance.

What did he learn from Witherspoon that would affect his view of political power?

"Interpreting Scripture and the script of human experience, Witherspoon spoke often about human nature...His view of human nature must be seen in relation to his view of the 'Dominion of Providence.' On the basis of this dependence, Witherspoon could emphasize human depravity as universal and inevitable without excluding or minimizing man's obvious potential for good. The latter possibility was evidence of the preserving providence of God, who was continually working to fulfill his promises and purposes."[5]

Because Madison gained a realistic Christian view of the nature of man from Dr. Witherspoon, he had far less confidence in the people than Jefferson did — far less confidence in political majorities.

"He steered clear of that optimism in human nature which almost always leads to anarchy, and thus he helped to modify the least desirable aspects of Jefferson's political thrust."[6]

It is not too much to assert, as Smylie does, that "Madison translated the views of Witherspoon on the nature of man into a political instrument."[7]

Virtue Essential

Because our system of representative government was created by godly men, like Madison and Witherspoon, it needs the leavening of godly men and women to make it work — whether acting as voters or as those elected to office. This is not to say that men must be perfect in order to have good government. Such a hope would be unrealistic. But men — and women — who understand and support the Biblical view of man and government are needed to represent the people at all levels of government. As Samuel Adams observed:

"He therefore is the truest friend to the liberty of his country who tries most to promote its virtue, and who, so far as his power and influence extend, will not suffer a man to be chosen into any office of power and trust who is not a wise and virtuous man....The sum of all is, if we would most truly enjoy this gift of Heaven, let us become a virtuous people..." (T&L, p. 247)

The Second Pillar of the Constitution: The Separation of Powers

Because our Founding Fathers realized that trusting too much authority to any one man or group of men was dangerous, they opposed *concentration* of power and favored its *distribution* or *dispersion.* The second pillar of the Constitution, therefore, is the separation of powers.

Our Founders really did not need the French philosopher, Charles de Montesquieu, to tell them that "in every government there are three sorts of power," for they already knew the source of these three powers. "For the Lord is our judge; the Lord is our lawgiver; the Lord is our King." (Isa. 33:22) They knew that human government should seek God's model for these three aspects of political power. But they were impressed by this eminent French philosopher's analysis of the need for a separation of powers and of the divine origin of all law and power in his *Spirit of Laws.*

"God is related to the universe, as Creator and Preserver; the laws by which He created all things are those by which He preserves them. He acts according to these rules, because He knows them; He knows them because He made them; and He made them, because they are in relation to His Wisdom and power..." (CHOC, p. 134)

Scriptural Guidelines and Limitations of Power

Certainly God knew what frame of government would best suit the frame of man. That is why He limits the power of civil government by His own authority. Throughout Scripture, there are numerous guidelines and limitations upon civil authorities. The absolute power and control God exercises over all spheres of government were never given by Him to any finite man or group of men who by their very nature would be incapable of exercising such awesome power justly. (See Gen. 9:1-6; Ezek. 45:9; Rom. 13:1-5; Rev. 1:5) Reasoning from this Biblical perspective, our Founders agreed with Montesquieu that

"When the legislative and executive powers are united in the same person, or in the same body of magistrates, there can be no liberty...There is no liberty, if the judiciary power be not separated from the legislative and executive. Were it joined with the legislative, the life and liberty of the subject would be exposed to arbitrary control; for the judge would be then the legislator. Were it joined to the executive power, the judge might behave with violence and oppression." (CHOC, p. 134-135)

Consequently, in the Federal Government, we find a careful separation of the three powers of government, none of which constitutionally has any right to encroach on the other. But, as Rosalie J. Slater reminds us:

"Can we expect these three governmental actions to operate correctly if we, as individual Christians, do not know the source from which they are derived, and what was their purpose? In our ignorance today we are tempted to believe that the power of the judicial, executive, and legislative branches of our government resides in those individuals who staff these offices. Yet, upon consideration of the Biblical base and purpose, we can see that the power or control resides not in the staffing but in the electorate which these offices represent. It resides in each individual Christian as he allows Christ to rule his life." (T&L, p. 242)

The Capacity of Mankind For Self-Government

We twentieth-century Americans have journeyed far from the principles of our Founding Fathers. No longer understanding our Constitution, we have allowed the human desire for unchecked power to circumvent constitutional law through executive orders, judicial decrees, or legislation that intrudes on the legitimate rights of the people. Today, most of our people believe that the Federal Government is an inevitable intruder into most areas of their lives simply because "we now live in such a complex society." Some even say we are no longer capable of self-government. What a tragedy if this should turn out to be true!

Our Founders knew that the sin nature of man required society to be protected from concentration of power in a few hands. But they also knew that man had been created in the image and likeness of God and that, with the aid of Divine Providence, he was capable of self-government. Thus James Madison wrote concerning the plan of government finally agreed upon at the Constitutional Convention:

"The first question that offers itself is whether the general form and aspect of the government be strictly republican. It is evident that no other form would be reconcilable with the genius of the people of America; with the fundamental principles of the Revolution; or with the honorable determination which animates every votary of freedom, to rest all our political experiments on the capacity of mankind for self-government."[8]

So it is that the integrity of all three powers of government depends upon the integrity of the self-governing individual and on what he acknowledges to be the foundation of the body politic – the Laws of God, or the laws of men.

The Third Pillar of the Constitution: A Dual Form of Government

The third pillar of the Constitution, our unique dual system of government, is America's solution to the age-old philosophical question: How can unity and diversity exist in harmony? How can there be individual liberty and also cultural and governmental unity without one destroying the other? Our Founders concluded that only through a balanced, Biblical perspective could they arrive at a form of government that allowed *both* form and freedom, unity and diversity. It was a difficult concept to grasp. John Fiske ascribes to "the great mind" of James Madison the honor of being the first

> *"to entertain distinctly the noble conception of two kinds of government operating at one and the same time upon the same individuals, harmonious with each other, but each supreme in its own sphere.*[9]

As we mentioned before, in both the Old and New Testaments civil government is always limited and accountability is demanded of representatives who exercise strictly delegated authority. (See Deut. 1:13; Exod. 18:21; Luke 20:25; Acts 1:19-20) From the Biblical perspective all human authority is delegated because God is sovereign. The concept of different spheres of authority acting upon the same individuals or, rather, proceeding from, the same individuals could only work in a Biblically-based society. In order to avoid the eventual usurpation of power by the strongest institution, there must be a recognition that God has delegated certain "unalienable rights" – and responsibilities – to specific institutions: the home, church, school, and state.

The Slavery Issue

While deciding how to determine the population of each state, the delegates came up against the issue of slavery. In their desire to present a united front to the world on the eve of Independence, the Continental Congress in 1776 had postponed handling this explosive issue. (Under the Confederation, however, it did abolish slavery in all areas north of the Ohio River. The states that developed in the great Northwest Territory were later admitted to the union as "free states" where slavery was not permitted.)

Now, at the Constitutional Convention, many voices were raised in favor of abolishing slavery everywhere in the Union. The great political leaders of Virginia – Washington, Madison, and Mason – were all opposed to slavery. But when it was proposed that slaves should be included in computing the population of the states, other voices were raised.

While the Northern states opposed including slaves in determining the ratio of representation, the Southern states wanted them included. In the end, a compromise was reached providing that three-fifths of the slaves should be counted for purposes of representation in Congress.

The Judgment of Heaven

Congress then debated the question of controlling interstate and international commerce. Again, the slavery issue arose. Charles Pickney and John Rutledge of South Carolina spoke up in favor of continuing the importation of slaves. At this point George Mason of Virginia could contain himself no longer. He rose and sternly warned his fellow delegates:

"Every master of slaves is born a petty tyrant. They bring the judgment of heaven upon a country. As nations cannot be rewarded or punished in the next world, they must be in this. By an inevitable chain of causes and effects, Providence punishes national sins by national calamities."[11]

It is tragic that Mason's timely warning went unheeded by a sufficient number of delegates. Again, this explosive issue was shelved. Congress gained the right to regulate the interstate and foreign commerce which had been causing so much friction between the states, but pro slavery forces achieved a deplorable victory: They succeeded in preventing Congress from even considering abolishing the importation of slaves until 1808!

The handling of the slavery issue was unquestionably a serious blot on the work of the Constitutional Convention which opened itself to divine direction in so many other ways and accomplished so much of enduring worth. It should serve as a reminder to us of what Madison and Witherspoon understood so well: the sin nature of man often prevents him from accomplishing all that God would have him do. But God is not mocked. Although it took a disastrous Civil War, His providence achieved the abolition of slavery through blood when it could so easily have been achieved by the pen. This episode is also a reminder that God did not bless our Founding Fathers merely because they were brilliant thinkers, but only to the extent that they relied upon Him – and in regard to slavery they did not. Nevertheless, our remarkable Constitution was brought into being owing to His providence.

Bill of Rights

The Constitution almost failed to be ratified by the states because of another fundamental defect: There was no Bill of Rights. George Mason and others at the Convention were sure that without careful spelling out of the individual's basic rights to his liberties, the central government might encroach on the rights of the individual. Madison promised to do all in his power to secure a Bill of Rights in exchange for ratification of the Constitution. He kept his promise. With ratification, America produced a unique political system: a dual form of government, the central government supreme in its sphere, and the state governments supreme in their spheres.

Rosalie J. Slater sees the Biblical basis of this dual form of government as derived from the Two Commandments of our Lord (Matt. 22:37-40):

> *"Our national sense, as Americans, is predicated upon our willingness to be God-governed – the first commandment. This is the basis for Christian Self-Government. Our federal sense, as Californians, Washingtonians, Oregonians, etc. – is predicated upon the second commandment. The individual's relation to God and to man are hereby stated, and for the Christian, there must be consistency in his behavior – whether he is dealing with one neighbor – or two hundred million."* (T&L, pp. 242-243)

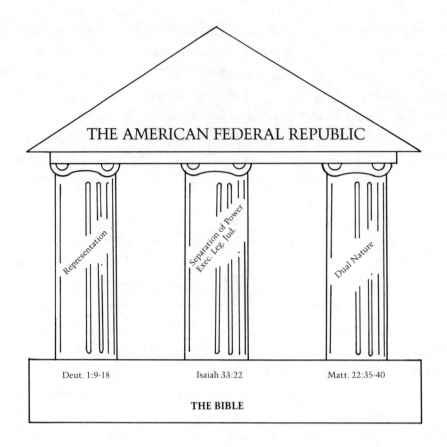

THE AMERICAN FEDERAL REPUBLIC

Representation

Separation of Power
Exec. Leg. Jud.

Dual Nature

Deut. 1:9-18   Isaiah 33:22   Matt. 22:35-40

THE BIBLE

Christianity Astonished the World

The representative system, the separation of powers, the dual form of government, these three great pillars of the American system of government, were the inspired means to that great end – the world's first Christian republic. As Verna Hall remarks:

> *"Each religion has a form of government, and Christianity astonished the world by establishing self-government. With the landing of the Pilgrims in 1620, Christian self-government became the foundation-stone of the United States of America. 'The stone which the builders refused is become the head stone of the corner.' (Ps. 118:22; Matt. 21:42)"* (CHOC, p. III)

In an election sermon in 1799, Dr. Jedediah Morse reminds us of our part in the preservation of our Christian form of government:

> *"To the kindly influence of Christianity we owe that degree of civil freedom, and political and social happiness which mankind now enjoy. In*

144

proportion as the genuine effects of Christianity are diminished in any nation, either through unbelief, or the corruption of its doctrines, or the neglect of its institutions; in the same proportion will the people of that nation recede from the blessings of genuine freedom...Whenever the pillars of Christianity shall be overthrown, our present republican forms of government, and all the blessings which flow from them, must fall with them." (CHOC, p. V)

Today we have the awesome but exhilarating task of repairing these pillars of Christianity which are also the pillars of our Constitution, that the structure shall not fall.

Colonizing Ideas

As we repair our own nation and put it in order, we shall then be in a position to do what we were meant to do originally – to "colonize ideas," specifically, the Christian idea of man and government so that it does not stop on these shores, but goes on to cover the globe. Our historians used to believe that it was part of our mission to colonize America's unique political ideas, but as we have forgotten what our Founding Father's achieved – forgotten the source of our freedom and affluence – we have failed to do this.

This does not mean that we can export our *structure* and *system* of government to other countries and expect it to make sense to them without an understanding of the Christian principles of self-government that underlie the structure. We have learned that self-government begins first with the individual aligning himself with the will of God, then caring for himself and others and applying Biblical principles to all areas of his life until he produces a civil government that reflects his godly self-government. All merely external forms of democratic structure which we may attempt to promote in other lands are doomed to failure and will inevitably bring cries of "American imperialism" or cries of an attempt to exercise external control over other nations.

Attempts to throw money at the acute problems in Africa and Latin America, when there is little understanding of Christian self-government in these lands, is a tragic waste of resources. If a fraction of the resources now spent on military hardware was spent on colonizing the ideas of our Founders, a proper foundation would be laid for the development of liberty and self-government in these lands.

The communists know the value of ideas and have for years been colonizing theirs which lead only to chaos and bondage. On the other hand, our political ideas, under the Providence of God, have achieved more civil and religious liberty and more self-government and genuine prosperity than the world has ever known before. We need to recapture the vision of the great American historian, Charles Bancroft, who wrote:

> *"America stands a model which other nations will carefully copy, in due time, as they can adapt themselves and change their institutions. There may be no literal copy or close formal imitation; but there is little doubt that the spirit and true sense of our Declaration of Independence will finally mould the structure and control the workings of all governments..."* (CHOC, p. 6)

Bancroft, writing in the nineteenth century, was optimistic about spreading the essence of our liberty. But he could not foresee that the American people would lose "the spirit and true sense of our Declaration of Independence...." He, like our Founding Fathers, understood that our form of government can only be communicated from the spirit of one people to the spirit of another. Good government – Biblical government – cannot be forced from without, but rises from within the hearts of a people.

Notes:

1. James Madison, *The Federalist*, No. 10 (New York: Tudor Publishing Co., 1937), p. 67
2. Ibid., p. 67-68.
3. Ibid., p. 68
4. James H. Smylie, "Madison and Witherspoon: Theological Roots of American Political Thought," *The Princeton University Library Chronicle* 22 (Spring 1961): p. 119
5. Ibid., p. 121.
6. Ibid., p. 131.
7. Ibid.
8. Madison, *The Federalist*, No. 39, p. 256.
9. Fiske, *Critical Period*, p. 239.
10. Ibid.
11. *The Papers of George Mason*, ed. Robert A. Rutland, 3 vols. (Chapel Hill, NC.: The University of North Carolina Press, 1970), 3:1787.

Further Reading – Chapter 7

Chapter 7 – Study Questions

1.   What did the Founding Fathers hope to achieve by the First Amendment to the Federal Constitution? _____

_____

2.   What are the three pillars of the American constitutional form of government? _____

_____

3.   What are some Biblical references to describe each form? _____

_____

4.   In what ways have the three pillars deteriorated? _____

_____

5.   What caused their deterioration? _____

_____

6.   Why is Christian character necessary to the maintenance of the American republic? _____

_____

7. How is our republic different from those of Greece and Rome? _____

_____

_____

8. Why is the election of Godly people as our representatives vital to the preservation of our unique republic? _____

_____

_____

9. What necessary qualities should our representatives possess? _____

_____

_____

10. What is the purpose of the separation of power? _____

_____

_____

11. Where does power lie – in us or in our representatives? _____

_____

_____

12. What was the great achievement of the Connecticut Compromise? _____

_____

_____

13. What will happen to our nation's form of government if its Christian foundation continues to be undermined? _____

_____

_____

14. How can we "colonize" the Christian idea of man and government? ___

_____

_____

Chapter 8

A Strategy for Success

"This book of the law shall not depart out of thy mouth; but thou shalt meditate therein day and night, that thou mayest observe to do all that is written therein: for then thou shalt make thy way prosperous, and then thou shalt have good success."

Joshua 1:8

THE SURRENDER OF YORKTOWN
OCTOBER 19, 1781
BY LOUIS VAN BLARENBERGHE

"I take a particular pleasure in acknowledging that the interposing Hand of Heaven, in the various instances of our extensive Preparation for this Operation [Yorktown], has been most conspicuous and remarkable."

George Washington to Thomas McKean,
President of Congress,
November 15, 1781

150

Chapter 8

A Strategy for Success

During the course of this study the authors have attempted to bring to light the untold story of "The American Covenant." This covenant is not one document, but a traceable chain of individual, church, and governmental agreements between the God of the Bible and the American people. We believe the American Covenant is the fundamental reason for the successful rise of our constitutional republic. The beguiling "father of lies" has for too long taken the day of battle as his messengers have distorted the facts of our history and omitted the reason for America's greatness. God told His people that they "perish for lack of knowledge" (Hosea 4:6), and so it is today, especially in the strategic battle for the American republic.

Throughout this book, many reasons have been given for the decline of our nation. But the purpose of this unveiling has not been to detail the failures of our modern secular state and its educational institutions. Ample material exists documenting the bankruptcy of the various secular alternatives that claim to have the solution to the crises of our time. (See John Whitehead's book, *The Stealing of America*, for a penetrating analysis of the current situation.)

The blame for our current perilous condition must fall upon those of us who say we believe in God and share the legacy of our Founders' vision. We have forfeited the institutions bequeathed to us by our forefathers. They have not been forcibly taken away from us by some overwhelming conspiracy, but we and our fathers simply stopped teaching the Bible's nation-building principles to ourselves and our children.

Now a new day is dawning. Americans are once again studying the power of God in our history. As a result, many are renewing their faith for the saving of our nation and are believing once again the words of our Lord: "The gates of hell shall not prevail against it [my church]." (Matt. 16:18)

Instant Replay

To this point we have outlined what America once was and what principles undergirded the structure of our republic. We have shown how the individual, once the Bible was in his hands, desired to be free from external dominance by either King or Pope. That individual then became self-governing in all areas and formed institutions (churches, schools, government) to protect the individual in order that he might serve God. ("Let my people go that they may serve me." Exodus 9:1) In Chapters 6 and 7 we illustrated how our Founders reasoned our economic and governmental establishments from a Biblical world-view that was commonly shared. Now, in this final chapter, let us analyze an historically proven strategy for success that can lead to the rebirth of our nation.

Planning to Win

Few of the philosophies planning to engulf the world have a reasonable hope of winning the battle for the minds of men. The Marxists are perhaps the most systematic and barbaric in their scheming for world dominance. Fanatical adherents of Islam also must be recognized for their sheer numbers and fervor in working toward an Islamic world. The third world-view capable of world domination is perhaps the most forgotten due to its apparent impotence. That philosophy is the Christian idea of man and government. Until the middle of the nineteenth century, the latter was the predominant force in the civilized world.

Hiding Behind Neutrality

One of the above philosophies, or religious world-views, will dominate our culture. It is surely the ultimate irrationalism to believe that a "do-your-own-thing" America will survive to the twenty-first century. A self-centered, materialistic democracy is no match for well-defined, war-tested, revolutionary ideas.

It has been the presupposition of this study that a proper understanding of Biblical Christianity, when lived out in the lives of individuals and institutions, has brought the greatest degree of liberty, prosperity, creativity and peace that the world has known. There have been aberrations of this truth as men, desiring to hide themselves behind the religious symbol of the Cross, have pillaged nations on so-called Crusades, put men in slavery, and persecuted Jews. But a perusal of history, as seen in this volume, shows that these atrocities do not represent the philosophy or methodology of Jesus and the Apostles or of true Christianity. The authentic Founder of Christianity never called for an external theocracy, but offered freely an internal transformation of life that would lead to external transformations of society and to a better life for all.

Not a Theocracy

Perhaps a note of clarification is needed at this point. The misconception is widespread that those, like ourselves, who believe that a return to Biblical principles in our society and government is imperative are, at the same time, calling for a legalistic theocracy that would destroy liberty and dictate religious views to the people. The source of such fears is somewhat understandable since there have been power hungry leaders throughout history who have used the Church as their excuse to persecute men (i.e., the so-called divine right of kings).

What we are calling for is a simple return to the principles laid down by our Founding Fathers in the Declaration of Independence and the Constitution. These documents, following the genuine Christian philosophy of freedom of choice, allowed the individual to determine his own faith and practice without governmental interference. Conscience was not to be *compelled.* The individual was to be left free to choose his faith or to have none at all. Nevertheless, this was not an invitation to hedonism. There had to be a basic code of law and societal standards; that code was found in the Bible. It acted not to repress the individual in his constructive activities – but to liberate the human being as never before. Nineteenth century historian Charles Bancroft summarized the positive impact of the early American republic upon all men:

> *"As the heart in the human body receives the current of blood from all parts of the system, and, having revitalized it, returns it with fresh elements of strength, so America adopts the children of all lands only to return a manhood ennobled by a sense of its own dignity through the practice of a system of self-government which improves the condition and promotes the interest of each while it produces harm to none."* (CHOC, p. 8)

No other nation in history has accepted those of varying faiths and creeds as has the United States of America. *Coercion* is not the Christian way, but *persuasion* and love ("Come now and let us reason together," Isa.

1:18). Our warning is to the Christian community, for if we do not *persuade* our fellow Americans through our loving words and actions of the necessity for maintaining our nation's Biblical roots, all of us – both believers and un-believers – will be led down the well-traveled path to slavery.

Winning the War, Not Just a Battle

If we are to avoid misconceptions mentioned above and succeed in restoring our nation, we must proceed carefully. Remember that only a very small minority of Americans (approximately 5%) "makes things happen" in our country. Mr. James Halcomb, the master planner of the Alaska Pipeline, who is one of the finest strategic planners in America, gives some invaluable insights concerning reaching a goal. Here are three aspects of that planning strategy:

1. We Must Know Our Goal!

As Christians, we should be in general agreement as to our goal, since we have the infallible Word of God to guide us in fulfilling God's will. But after helping many Christian organizations, Mr. Halcomb has found that this is not always the case. Many, he says, have no observable goal and so reach no observable objective.

Now is a good time to reflect upon whether we have set our life goals in line with God's ultimate purpose to be glorified in all things. (I Pet. 4:11) Twentieth-century Christianity has often encouraged a self-centered goal relating to personal fulfillment, rather than a God-centered goal which accomplishes His cosmic purpose. We have too often been subtly caught by the "me oriented" world view and therefore have not seen ourselves as a vital part of the army of God marching through history with a common commission.

As mentioned in the introduction to this book, a few socialists shared the ideal of a "perfect socialist state" and were nearly able to derail the "prodigal nation of America" by offering the people a goal of sorts.

If an historically disastrous scheme can gain such influence, what will be the impact when millions of Americans reaffirm the American Covenant "to the glory of God and the advancement of the Christian faith"? The slowdown in the cultural impact of Christianity in the twentieth century is not because other philosophies are better or stronger, but because God's people have forgotten and not pursued His goal with a passion to see it accomplished!

2. We Must Know Our Assets

Jesus said that before we embark upon any venture we should count the cost and see that we have the needed materials to carry out the task. (Luke 14:28) If this book has attempted to communicate anything, it is that the most powerful asset for accomplishing God's purpose that has ever been known to the world is the self-governing Christian in covenant with his God.

Our Forgotten Gold Mine

We have seen how God set the stage for the full functioning of this world-changing individual and how Jesus Christ died to set the individual free from the burden of sin. He told His disciples "greater works than these shall you do, because I go to the Father." (John 14:12) Then we recalled how He gave to His new creation His Spirit and a completed Word to guide him into all truth. We traced how the individual was set free from the bondage of statism when the Bible made its way to the common man, so that he could express his Christian self-government in every area of life, without the state dictating his every move. We saw how a nation was prepared that protected the rights of the individual so that he could accomplish God's purpose.

As we enter this critical stage in the battle for the Gospel of Christ, are most American Christians aware of the great assets which have been given to them as a result of the faith of millions of persecuted believers over 2,000 years? Is it not our responsibility to use and preserve what God has given us more than those who have never shared such a heritage? Jesus said, "To whom much is given, much is required." (Luke 12:48)

The Art of Nation-Building

During our study, we have discovered that our Founders were Biblicists who believed that the Word of God was the foundation to success in all areas. Let us illustrate the art of nation-building that they left for us and compare it with the humanist model.

155

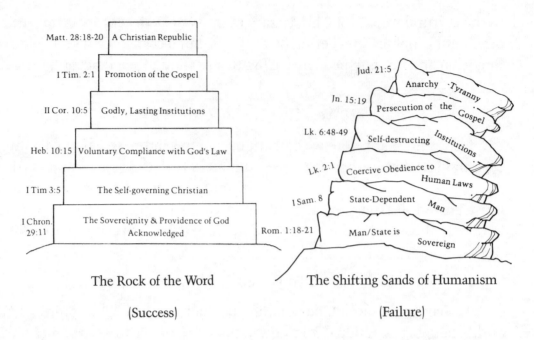

Matt. 28:18-20	A Christian Republic
I Tim. 2:1	Promotion of the Gospel
II Cor. 10:5	Godly, Lasting Institutions
Heb. 10:15	Voluntary Compliance with God's Law
I Tim 3:5	The Self-governing Christian
I Chron. 29:11	The Sovereignty & Providence of God Acknowledged

The Rock of the Word

(Success)

Jud. 21:5 Anarchy · Tyranny

Jn. 15:19 Persecution of the Gospel

Lk. 6:48-49 Self-destructing Institutions

Lk. 2:1 Coercive Obedience to Human Laws

I Sam. 8 State-Dependent Man

Rom. 1:18-21 Man/State is Sovereign

The Shifting Sands of Humanism

(Failure)

Comparing the two diagrams above and their techniques of nation-building, which of them do you think is more likely to succeed? We live in a day in which many Americans cower in fear believing the unbiblical and ungodly system shown above is going to sweep the world while, in reality, it is doomed to eventual self-destruction. If we can restore our nation's Biblical foundations, civil and religious liberty also will be restored. Our success as a nation is not dependent upon any external power.

In order to reach our goal of re-establishing self- and civil government, should we spend our priority time combatting the collapsing tent of humanism, or rebuilding our godly system? Our critiques of the humanist system can accomplish little beyond awakening the people, but an example of a positive Christian alternative will have assured results, because light always dispels darkness. Building upon our assets, which requires knowing our true history, we can once again be a light on a hill, becoming an example to other nations, rather than a reproach.

3. We Must Know the Critical Path

In strategic planning, "the critical path" is a term often used to describe the chain of critical or important events that *must* take place to accomplish a goal. For example, the building of a guided missile involves hundreds of steps and processes. If someone forgets to place a decal on the side of the missile, it may be somewhat inconsequential, but if, while constructing the missile, a fuel line is not included, then the million-dollar nose cone will never get off the ground.

156

Most people do not follow a critical path to accomplish their life goal. The "urgent" or "emergency" path method is much more common (e.g., answering every telephone call, putting out fires in the office, etc.) This technique abandons planning to circumstance and focuses upon the so-called "urgent" issue of the moment without regard to what is important in the long run.

Jesus taught the method to be used to accomplish His great goals. His was not the "emergency path" method. He had a critical path that He followed throughout His life, not allowing Himself to be sidetracked by circumstances (Luke 13:31-33).

He knew the Kingdom of Heaven would grow in the hearts of men and then would influence all of society, but it was not to be a bloody revolution of the flesh. (Matt. 26:51-54), but an infiltrating or leavening from within. (See the parables on the Kingdom in Matthew 13.) The method, or critical path, of Jesus was to make right the *internal* (change the hearts of men), then the *external* results (liberty, justice, love) would follow.

You may have noticed that this guide does not focus mainly upon the *issues* of the day, but upon the *principles* behind them. For from the heart comes the issues of life (Prov. 4:23). *Ideas have consequences.* If Christians in America will learn to reason from principles (ideas) to the issues of life (consequences) then they will be ready for battle and for victory.

Unfortunately today, millions of Christians are hurtling into the issues of the day without a firm foundation of principles and an understanding of history. Their efforts are frustrated because they have left God's critical path.

Internal to the External

God's critical path for the rebuilding of our nation begins with the self-governing Christian. A godly nation is not simply prayed for and received; it is built "line upon line, precept upon precept" (Is. 28:10). The self-governing Christian is God's building-block for a Christian nation.

In Scripture, the Christian is seen as more than a person who does good and avoids evil. He has within him all the power necessary to bring all areas of life into submission to God, which is his ordained purpose (I Cor. 10:31; II Cor. 10:5). See the diagram below. United with the Word of God and faith, he will accomplish all that His Lord has commanded (Ps. 8:3-6)

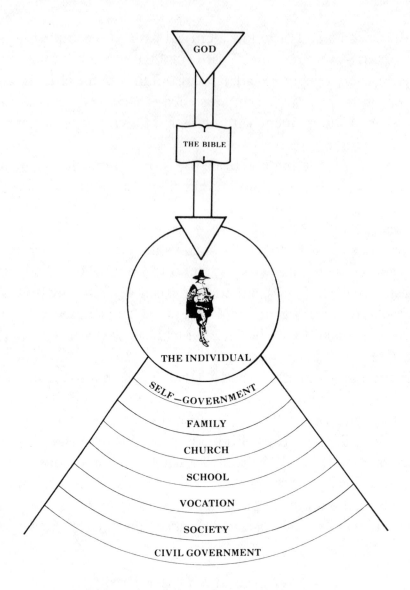

GOD

THE BIBLE

THE INDIVIDUAL

SELF—GOVERNMENT

FAMILY

CHURCH

SCHOOL

VOCATION

SOCIETY

CIVIL GOVERNMENT

Expanding Spheres of Influence

If you agree with the premise of this book, then your desire is to move forward practically to see the realization of the goal stated by Daniel Webster, echoing our Pilgrim Fathers:

"Finally, let us not forget the religious character of our origin. Our fathers were brought hither by their high veneration for the Christian religion. They journeyed by its light, and labored in its hope. They sought to incorporate its principles with the elements of their society, and to diffuse its influence through all their institutions, civil, political, or literary. Let us cherish these sentiments, and extend this influence still more widely; in the full conviction, that that is the happiest society

which partakes in the highest degree of the mild and peaceful spirit of Christianity." (CHOC, p. 248)

As we go about accomplishing this task, we must build a firm foundation for the reformation of the structure of society. External changes based on power politics or heated rhetoric will be shortlived.

Ruling Our Own Spirit

Proverbs 25:28 says: "He that hath no rule (dominion) over his own spirit is like a city that is broken down, and without walls." If we cannot rule ourselves, our cities will certainly break down and, in their chaos, will eat up our liberty.

In 1654 Hugo Grotius beautifully stated the pattern of societal rule beginning with the rule of God in the individual:

"He knows not how to rule a kingdome, that cannot manage a Province; nor can he wield a Province, that cannot order a City; nor he order a City, that knows not how to regulate a Village; nor he a Village, that cannot guide a Family; nor can that man Govern well a Family that knows not how to Govern himselfe; neither can any Govern himselfe unless his reason be Lord, Will and Appetite her Vassals: nor can Reason rule unlesse herselfe be ruled by God, and (wholy) be obedient to Him." (T&L, p. 69)

Our Pilgrim fathers and our colonial forefathers both understood that dependence upon God was the only true insurance that the sin nature of man could be restrained and his great potential for good unleashed. If you are reading this book and do not know the God of our fathers, we hope you will see the necessity of coming to know Him through faith in His Son Jesus Christ. "If the Son therefore shall set you free, you shall be free indeed." (John 8:36)

The Self-Governing Christian Home

The most important institution for the saving and preserving of the world is the family. The destruction of the family, as we are witnessing in this generation is a sure sign of impending cultural collapse.

The self-governing home was the major institutional cornerstone of early America and for a study of this fact the reader should turn to pages 3-37 of *Teaching and Learning America's Christian History* and ponder the duties and impact of the American Christian home – the engine of godly dominion and the hope of the future for our nation.

God ordained the family institution in Genesis, Chapter 1, and through-out the Bible He enumerates the responsibilities of this unit for the care of its members (1 Tim. 5:8), the education and training of its children (Prov. 22:6) and for the purpose of stewardship and tithing to God's work on earth (II Cor. 16:2).

Suggestions for Home Government

The home has become a revolving door for most Americans where money, food, and TV time are provided. We must recapture and rebuild our homes.

The first area to reclaim is the education of our youth. In this century, we have been misled into believing that the public school is as innately American as the flag, mom, and apple pie. As parents, we must face the facts that tell us that "public schools" have become "statist schools" where the philosophy and the religion of the state are promoted. The uniqueness of America was, and should be again, that parents can educate their children in the religious and moral values of their choice. This is only possible, however, through privately-controlled and funded schools where parental control can be maintained.

If the parents who are reading this book would come to grips with the sacrificial decision to send their children to quality Bible-based private schools, the battle for our nation would be well on the road to victory. We know this is a challenging task, especially since many Christian schools are not the quality they should be. But there is no alternative. We as families must encourage the development of Christian schools. We who have the means must develop scholarship funds to help those who cannot afford private education.

To make this godly movement fulfil its purpose, parents should insist that these schools not only provide Christian teachers and Chapel services but a Bible-based curriculum in all subjects. (Many times schools unwittingly use secular humanist textbooks and methodology.) That curriculum should reflect the godly educational philosophy of our Founding Fathers and the training of our youth to be self-governing citizens of this great land. (Write us for further information on the early American "Principle Approach" to education.)

Along with education and care of our children, the home must become — if it is to follow the Biblical pattern — the place of hospitality once again. Only when the American homes and pocketbooks open to the needs of the elderly, handicapped and orphaned will the burden of federal taxation be lifted from our necks. Welfare is a family and church responsibility and so it remained in the United States well into the twentieth century.

A final suggestion for our homes is to make them training centers for our own personal study and for others in our communities. In early America, almost every home had a well-used library. Many of us may say, "How can I find the time? This sounds too difficult." *We have no choice.* We have passed the buck for too long. If we do not *read* and *think* governmentally, education-ally, economically, etc., someone else will do our thinking and decision-mak-ing for us!

We are encouraging the development of home institutes throughout America. Family and community training does not have to take place only in a convention center or college classroom, but right in our own homes as we turn off our TV sets and prepare ourselves for the battle of ideas. Write to us for information on curriculum, and videotapes available for your home institute.

We must teach our children the sacrifice of our fathers that ensured our liberty and the Providence of God in the founding of our nation in order to give them hope for the future. Out of homes that are willing to take the above suggestions seriously will come the future leaders of America who will more closely resemble the great statesmen of our Founding Father generation.

The Self-Governing Church

The believing church in America makes up almost 200,000 individual organizations. These churches of many different denominations were once the mainstay of every community and its activities. Now there is a growing realization that these local fellowships are the key to rebuilding our nation and reaffirming our covenant with God. (See "The American Christian Church," T&L, pp. 3-37)

The beginning of any action emanating from the local church should be a training of the congregation for their task in the world. Many fine churches are doing this and are encouraging study groups or Sunday School classes in our Christian heritage and its Biblical base. The book you are reading is being used in hundreds of churches for that purpose and there is a *Study Leader's Guide* available upon request for group study.

Self-Governing Christian Enterprise

We mentioned at the beginning of this chapter that the self-governing Christian is more than a person who is self-controlled. When seen in the sphere of economics, the self-governing individual is in reality neither an economic unit, as Marx called man, nor a creature of self-interest, as Adam Smith postulated. When properly prepared with God's principles of property and stewardship, the Christian believer is the most productive resource in the world. In past history he has been the driving force behind the industrial revolution and the great American prosperity that flowed from Reformation principles. Today, his role is more important than ever, for as he obeys God's principles of economics and learns how to be a godly entrepreneur, wisely investing what God has given him, he can provide the financial base needed to restore our land and take the gospel to the world (Luke 19:12-27)

Suggestions for Christian Enterprise

Here, as in other areas, we must escape the tendency to think that the Federal Reserve, "the government," or the big money brokers control our economic destiny. It is up to us to restore economic sanity to our nation through our example. We need to examine the Christian position on deficit spending, the graduated income tax, loaning our money to our nation's enemies, government regulation of business, etc. Then, we need to band together with others to promote godly answers that will give us assured economic success. (Deut. 28). We must resist governmental efforts to control business, steal our property, and drive us to dependence upon its "merciful" handouts.

When he came to America in the 1830's, Alexis De Tocqueville said he saw very little evidence of external government, but that the nation seemed to be run by voluntary associations. Most of these associations that cared for the needs of society were tithing associations (Christian ministries), either related to a church or started by some Christian and supported by tithing Christians. Average voluntary giving to charity is way down today. Instead of giving 10% or so to God, we now give almost one-half of our incomes to the government. Until we have made up our giving to God, we should expect to carry this double burden. (Malachi 3)

If even a fraction of today's 100 million or so church-goers begin to tithe to godly causes, in and out of the church, then billions of dollars will be released to show forth the love of God, and the role of the Federal government will immediately begin to shrink to its proper size. Christian schools, hospitals, businesses, and social agencies can offer real examples of Christian love. Christian "think tanks" or study centers can open up principles and historically proven solutions to society's problems. The impact of applying the above ideas will overwhelm the secular humanist (through love, not criticism – knowledge, not reactionary emotionalism) showing to the world what God can do through individuals committed to Him.

Our Self-Governing Republic

There is increasing discussion today, even in Washington, of restoring our self-governing republic. The only possible way for such rhetoric to become a reality is if the critical path we have just discussed is followed. We have left discussion of civil government to the end, not because it is the least important area of our lives, but to emphasize that the basic structure of government will not conform to its original constitutional model until the people become self-governing in their homes, churches, schools and businesses.

Suggestions for Good Government

We must also begin immediately to become involved in the political process, for there are issues that need to be confronted before our entire structure is destroyed. For example, God will not long tolerate a nation that legally kills the unborn child calling it "abortion." Let us remember that a very small percentage of people is involved in the political process except when they vote, and only a minority even bother to vote. We have inherited peaceful and lawful means of reform and we have no right to speak of civil disobedience when we have not used our constitutional means of redressing grievances.

It is a fatal mistake to forget that the godly way of nation-building presupposes as its foundation godly character and intelligent self-governing people. This is the reason we are failing in our current attempt to set up republics in foreign lands. It does little good to give a copy of the Constitution and plans for popular elections to a people who do not know how to govern themselves. The battle must be won from the *internal* to the *external*, from content to form, from character to its full expression as a Christian republic.

The governmental applications for the principles in this book are many. One basic theme that should be driven home through letters, discussion, and political pressure is that civil government in America must shrink to its Biblical and Constitutional function, i.e., to protect the lives, liberties and estates of the citizens "...that we may lead a quiet and peaceable life in all godliness and honesty." (I Tim. 2:2)

Many of us need to train for public service, in this way ensuring that the God-intended purpose for magistrates is fulfilled. (Rom. 13) We cannot expect ungodly men to lead our nation toward our Founding Fathers' perception of a republic. If humanists maintain leadership, Christians will soon be the outcasts of society and civil liberty will be but a memory. "When the righteous are in authority, the people rejoice: but when the wicked beareth rule, the people mourn." (Prov. 29:2)

Is There Real Hope?

Even after seeing the potential means of restoration, the well-informed reader may rightly ask at this point, "Is there a real hope for meaningful cultural change?" We have traveled far down the road from our Biblical origins. Certainly, short-term, pragmatic measures to reform the economy, halt our moral decline, and reverse the flood of government incursion into our lives will not stop the tide of totalitarianism that is sweeping our world.

Alexander Solzhenitsyn, in his acceptance speech for the Templeton Prize for Progress in Religion (May 1983) summarized our present state well when he said:

"We are witnesses to the devastation of the world, be it imposed or voluntarily undergone. The entire twentieth century is being sucked into the vortex of atheism and self-destruction. This plunge into the abyss has aspects that are unquestionably global, dependent neither on political systems, nor on levels of economic and cultural development, nor yet on national pecularities. And contemporary Europe, seemingly so unlike the Russia of 1913, is today on the verge of the same collapse...Different parts of the world have followed different paths, but today they are all approaching the threshold of a common ruin."

Today's world has reached the stage which, if it had been described in the preceding centuries, would have called for the cry: "This is the Apocalypse!"

So what hope is there? To be honest, if we live in a world without God, there is very little hope. But if, as we declare in this book, a loving God "presides over the affairs of men," great reformation can and usually does occur in times of great distress.

Speaking as a Christian, Solzhenitsyn ends his sobering address in London by challenging us to remember God and reform our world.

"Instead of the ill-advised hopes of the last two centuries, which have reduced us to insignificance and brought us to the brink of nuclear and non-nuclear death, we can only reach with determination for the warm hand of God, which we have so rashly and self-confidently pushed away. If we did this, our eyes would be opened to the errors of this unfortunate twentieth century and our hands could be directed to set them right.

There is nothing else to cling to in the landslide: all the thinkers of the Enlightenment can give us nothing.

"Our five continents are caught in a whirlwind. But it is during such trials that the highest gifts of the human spirit are manifested. If we perish and lose this world, the fault will be ours alone."

Success in "The Worst of Times"!

Throughout our historical survey we have highlighted the fact that real world-changers are not defeated by bleak circumstances, but overcome them. Our patriot forefathers were such men and their example can be a great lesson for us on the way of success – even in the worst of times.

On January 1, 1781 things looked bleak in the patriot cause. The Pennsylvania line troops had revolted for lack of pay and short enlistments. The reason for no pay was that the continental paper money had collapsed and was "not worth a continental." The Army had to live off the land and barter for its needs. Washington, who took no salary for his efforts, did not even have sufficient funds to entertain foreign dignitaries when soliciting their help. This war with one of the great world powers had gone on for eight full years and at the beginning of 1781 it was the worst of times.

The parallels to our time, two hundred years later, are obvious. We face an awesome military machine, our economy is built upon a precariously balanced paper currency no more sound than the early Continental, and the morale of our people to fight a protracted war (especially a battle for the minds of men) is very low.

But let us now survey the events that brought the American cause from defeat to victory at Yorktown, Virginia on October 19, 1781.

Well-Laid Cosmic Plan

Led by George Morgan, the Americans defeated Colonel Tarleton's entire detachment at the Battle of the Cowpens, January 17, 1781. Lord Cornwallis, leading the large British army in the south, was infuriated by this defeat. Destroying his heavy baggage, he headed for the Catawba River to cut off the retreat of the small American army.

Cornwallis reached the Catawba River just two hours after General Morgan had crossed. Confident of victory, the British general decided to wait until morning to cross. But during the night a storm filled the river detaining his troops. Twice more in the next ten days Cornwallis nearly overtook the American Army. On Feburary 3, he reached the Yadkin River in North Carolina, just as the Americans were landing on the eastern slopes. But, before he could cross, a sudden flood cut off the British troops again! On February 13, the Americans reached the Dan River that would lead them into friendly Virginia territory. They crossed and a few hours later, when Cornwallis arrived, rising waters once again stopped him from defeating the American Army. Even Clinton, the commander-in-chief of Lord Cornwallis, acknowledged that Divine Providence had intervened. He wrote: "...here the royal army was again stopped by a sudden rise of the waters, which had only just fallen (almost miraculously) to let the enemy over, who could not else have eluded Lord Cornwallis' grasp, so close was he upon their rear..."[1]

The significance of the Battle of Cowpens and the safe retreat of the patriots that followed is that our small army in the south was saved by God's providence so that it could harass General Cornwallis and drive him to the sea, which set the stage for the final defeat of the British at Yorktown in October 1781.

Interposing Hand of Heaven

The above providential account is but one of many events that converged like parts of a well-laid cosmic plan to defeat the British. For example:

1. If General Washington had not decided to leave New York and march to Yorktown when he did, Cornwallis would have been reinforced.

2. If Robert Morris, the generous and capable merchant, had not used extraordinary means to raise money to pay Washington's troops, they would have gone home rather than to Yorktown.

3. If France had not sent a fleet from the West Indies (unknown to Washington) which arrived just in time to defeat the British fleet sent to relieve General Cornwallis at Yorktown, Cornwallis could have escaped. In this battle the French fleet, under Admiral De Grasse, soundly defeated the British cutting off all sea routes.

4. If a sudden tornado-like storm had not stopped Lord Cornwallis in his last-minute attempt on October 16, 1781 to cross the York River

and escape to New York, the war would have dragged on.

After the surrender at Yorktown, General Washington acknowledged the many providential events of the war. He declared the day after the surrender to be a day of Thanksgiving and his troops were directed to attend religious services. On November 15, 1781, Washington wrote to the President of Congress:

> *"I take a particular pleasure in acknowledging that the interposing hand of Heaven, in the various instances of our extensive preparations for this operation, has been most conspicuous and remarkable."*[1]

If Then, Why Not Now?

The "interposing hand of heaven" should be just as obvious to us today as it was to our Founders. They consistently declared church, town, state, and national days of prayer, humiliation and fasting. They knew that the nations were being sifted by the Hand of God and they understood periods of calamity, hardship, drought or blessing as important times to align themselves with the will of God. By repenting and acknowledging God in their history, our forefathers were reaffirming the American Covenant. What is to keep us from such a reaffirmation? Only if we are willing to have the faith of our fathers are we going to be able to restore the nation they built. Trusting in Him who is master of all, we can follow His strategy for success.

Conclusion

We have explained as best we can the untold story of "The American Covenant." A group of Christians met together off the coast of New England, covenanting with their God to form a nation that would glorify Him and spread His Gospel. They were followed by many others, most of whom reaffirmed and restated their initial compact. Out of their covenant with God and their willingness to apply His Word to all areas of life came a Christian republic that has promoted the greatest expansion of the Gospel in the history of man. We must now realize that we can no longer live off the heritage and covenant of our fathers. We must reaffirm their covenant and move ahead to become the Pilgrims of the 20th century, bearing the cross if we intend to wear the crown.

Our founders did not claim to have all the truth. They did not have the Biblical study aids we have. They did not have a Christian republic upon which to base their efforts. They did not have hours every day free from toil to use for study. But they did have a vision, a future orientation. They saw themselves standing upon the shoulders of the saints of the past. They knew there were greater things yet to come.

Listen to pastor John Robinson's farewell address to the Pilgrims as related by Pilgrim Edward Winslow. It was just before the Mayflower set sail from England for the New World.

> *"Here also he put us in mind of our church covenant, at least that part of it whereby we promise and covenant with God and one another to receive whatsoever light or truth shall be made known to us from His written Word; but withal exhorted us to take heed what we receive for truth, and well to examine and compare it and weigh it with other scriptures of truth before we receive it. For saith he, it is not possible the Christian world should come so lately out of such thick anti-Christian darkness, and that full prefection of knowledge break forth at once."*
> (CHOC, p. 184)

God surely has given us further light. Let us take His Word and truth to the four corners of the world so that we may hasten the day when "the earth shall be full of the knowledge of the Lord, as the waters cover the sea" (Is. 11:9)

Notes:

1. "Remember our Bicentennial – 1781," by William Hosmer, Foundation for Christian Self-Government *Newsletter* (June 1981), p. 5.
2. Writings of George Washington, Vol. 23, p. 343.

Chapter 8 – Study Questions

1. How should Christians determine their life goals? _____
_____

_____

2. What are some of the responsibilities of parents in the education of their children? _____
_____

_____

3. How can your church be more effective in meeting society's social problems? _____

_____

_____

4. Why is tithing so important? _____

_____

_____

5. What was the original source of American prosperity? _____

_____

_____

6. What values should be reflected by the Christian's vocation and lifestyle?

_____

_____

_____

7. What can we do to restore the structure of the American Christian republic? _____

_____

_____

8. Why do we need to focus on principles before issues? _____

_____

_____

9. What is the Biblical position on "deficit spending" and taxation? _____

_____

_____

10. What kind of voluntary associations should we institute and support? _

_____

11. Why do we need to reaffirm the American Covenant? _____

_____

_____

Selected Bibliography

Arber, Edward, ed. *The Story of The Pilgrim Fathers, 1606-1623, A.D., As Told by Themselves, their Friends and their Enemies.* London: Ward and Downey Limited; Boston and New York: Houghton, Mifflin & Co., 1897; reprint ed., New York: Klaus Reprint Co., 1969.

Baldwin, Alice M. *The New England Clergy and The American Revolution.* New York: Frederick Ungar Publishing Co., 1958.

Bartlett, Robert Merrill. *The Pilgrim Way.* Philadelphia: United Church Press, 1971.

Billington, D. W. *Patterns in History.* Donners Grove, Illinois: Inter-Varsity Press, 1979.

Bradford, William. *The History of Plymouth Plantation.* 2 vols. New York: Russell and Russell, 1968; reprint of 1st ed., Massachusetts Historical Society, 1856.

Brown, Alexander. *The Genesis of the United States.* Boston and New York: Houghton Mifflin & Co., 1890.

Brown, John. *The Pilgrim Fathers of New England and Their Puritan Successors.* Pasadena, Texas: Pilgrim Publications, 1970.

Burgess, Walter. *The Pastor of the Pilgrims, A Biography of John Robinson.* New York: Harcourt, Brace & Howe, 1920.

Burrage, Champlin. *The True Story of Robert Browne (1550?-1633), Father of Congregationalism.* London: Henry Frowde, 1906.

Campbell, Douglas. *The Puritan in Holland, England, and America.* New York: Harper & Bros., 1893.

Campbell, Norine Dickson. *Patrick Henry: Patriot and Statesman.* New York: The Devin-Adair Co., 1969.

Cornelison, Isaac A. *The Relation of Religion to Civil Government in the United States of America, a State without a Church, But Not without a Religion.* New York and London: G. P. Putnam & Sons, 1895.

d'Aubigne, J. H. Merle. *The Reformation in England.* Vol. 1. Carlisle, Pennsylvania: The Banner of Truth Trust, 1977.

Dexter, Henry Martyn and Dexter, Morton. *The England and Holland of the Pilgrims.* Boston: Houghton, Mifflin & Co., 1905.

Donovan, Frank. *Mr. Jefferson's Declaration.* New York: Dodd, Mead & Co., 1968.

Elazar, Daniel J. *From Biblical Covenant to Modern Federalism: The Federal Theology Bridge.* Philadelphia: Workshop on Covenant and Politics of the Center for the Study of Federalism, Temple University, 1980.

Fiske, John. *The American Revolution.* 2 vols. Boston and New York: Houghton, Mifflin & Co., 1898.

Fiske, John. *The Beginnings of New England or The Puritan Theocracy in Its Relations to Civil and Religious Liberty.* Boston and New York: Houghton, Mifflin & Co., 1900.

Fiske, John. *The Critical Period of American History: 1783-1789.* Boston and New York: Houghton, Mifflin & Co., 1898.

Green, J. R. *A Short History of The English People.* New York and London: Harper & Bros., 1898.

Hall, Verna M., Comp. *The Christian History of the American Revolution: Consider and Ponder.* San Francisco: Foundation for American Christian Education, 1975.

Hall, Verna M., Comp. *The Christian History of the Constitution of the United States of America: Christian Self-Government.* American Revolution Bicentennial Edition. San Francisco: Foundation for American Christian Education, 1975.

Hall, Verna M., Comp. *The Christian History of the Constitution of the United States of America: Christian Self-Government with Union.* San Francisco: Foundation for American Christian Education, rev. ed., 1979.

Hamilton, Alexander; Jay, John; Madison, James. *The Federalist.* New York: Tudor Publishing Co., 1937.

Henry, Matthew. *Commentary on the Whole Bible.* 6 vols. Old Tappan, N.J.: Fleming H. Revell Company. Reprint of 1721 edition.

Humanist Manifestos I and II. Buffalo, New York: Prometheus Books, 1977.

Johnson, William J. *George Washington, The Christian.* Milford, Michigan: Mott Media, 1976.

Kuiper, B. K. *The Church in History.* Grand Rapids, Michigan: The National Union of Christian Schools and William B. Eerdmans Publishing Company, 1978.

Latourette, Kenneth Scott. *A History of Christianity.* Vol 2: A.D. 1500-A.D. 1975. Revised edition. New York, Hagerstown, San Francisco, London: Harper & Row, Publishers, 1952. Paperback.

Locke, John. *The Reasonableness of Christianity As Delivered in the Scrip-*

tures. Edited and Introduced by George W. Ewing. A Gateway Edition. Chicago: Henry Regnery Company, 1965.

Locke, John. *Two Treatises of Government*. A Critical Edition with Introduction and Criticus Apparatus by Peter Laslett. Cambridge University Press, 1960; paperback edition, New York & Toronto: The New American Library, 1965.

Marshall, Peter, and Manuel, David. *The Light and the Glory*. Old Tappan, New Jersey: Fleming H. Revell Co., 1977.

Mason, George. *The Papers of George Mason*. 3 vols. Robert A. Rutland, ed. Chapel Hill, N.C.: The University of North Carolina Press, 1970.

McLaughlin, Andrew C. *The Foundations of American Constitutionalism*. New York: New York University Press, 1932; Fawcett World Library, 1961.

Miller, Perry. *The New England Mind: The Seventeenth Century*. New York: The MacMillan Company, 1939; Beacon Press, 1968.

Morison, Samuel Eliot, *Builders of The Bay Colony*. 2d ed., revised and enlarged. Boston: Houghton, Mifflin Co., 1958.

Neal, Daniel. *The History of the Puritans*. 5 vols. London: Richard Hett, 1732.

Neill, Edward D. *History of the Virginia Company of London*. Albany, New York: Joel Munsell, 1869.

Oberholtzer, Ellis Paxson. *Robert Morris, Patriot and Financier*. New York: The Macmillan Company, 1903.

Powell, Edward A., and Rushdoony, Rousas John. *Tithing and Dominion*. Vallecito, California: Ross House Books, 1979.

Prince, Thomas. *The Salvations of God in 1746*. Boston: D. Henchman, 1746.

Robinson, John. *The Works of John Robinson*. 3 vols. London: John Snow, 1851.

Rushdoony, Rousas John. *Revolt Against Maturity*. Fairfax, Virginia: Thoburn Press, 1977.

Rutland, Robert A. *George Mason: Reluctant Statesman*. Colonial Williamsburg, Inc., Holt, Rinehart and Winston, 1961.

Schaff, Philip. *History of the Christian Church*. VIII vols. Grand Rapids, Michigan: William B. Eerdmans Publishing Co., 1978.

Schaeffer, Francis A. *A Christian Manifesto*. Westchester, Illinois: Crossway Books, 1982.

Schaeffer, Francis A. *Escape from Reason*. Donner's Grove, Illinois: Inter-Varsity Press, 1968.

Schroeder, John Frederick, D.D., ed. *Maxims of Washington*. 5th ed. Mount Vernon, Virginia: The Mount Vernon Ladies' Association, 1974.

Selby, John. *The Road to Yorktown*. New York: St. Martin's Press, 1976.

Shafer, Paul W. and Snow, John Howland. *The Turning of the Tides*. New Canaan, Conn.: The Long House, 1962.

Slater, Rosalie J. *Teaching and Learning America's Christian History*. American Revolution Bicentennial Edition. San Francisco, California: Foundation for American Education, 1975.

Smith, Bradford. *Bradford of Plymouth*. Philadelphia and New York: J. B. Lippincott Co., 1951.

Smith, Bradford. *Captain John Smith, His Life and Legend*. Philadelphia and New York: J. B. Lippincott Company, 1953.

Smith, H. Sheldon, Handy, Robert T., and Loetscher, Lefferts A. *American Christianity: An Historical Interpretation with Representative Documents*. Vol. 1, 1607-1820. New York: Charles Scribner's Sons, 1960.

Smith, James Ward and Jamison, A. Leland, eds. *Religion in American Life*. Vol. 1: *The Shaping of American Religion*. Princeton: Princeton University Press, 1961.

Smith, John, Captain. *The General Historie of Virginia, New England and The Summer Isles* in *Travels and Works of Captain John Smith*. 2 vols. Edited by Edward Arber. Edinburgh: John Grant, 1910.

Smylie, James H. "Madison and Witherspoon: Theological Roots of American Political Thought," *The Princeton University Library Chronicle* 22, Spring 1981.

Stith, William. *The History of the First Discovery and Settlement of Virginia*. New York: Joseph Sabin Reprint, 1865; from 1st ed., Williamsburg, Virginia, 1747.

Tanner, J. R. *Constitutional Documents of the Reign of James I, A.D. 1603-1625*. Cambridge, England: Cambridge University Press, 1930.

Tocqueville, Alexis de. *Democracy in America*. 2 vols. Translated by Henry Reeve and revised by Francis Bowen. Edited by Phillips Bradley. New York: Alfred A. Knopf, Inc., 1945; paperback ed., New York: Vintage Books, Inc., 1955.

Whitehead, John W. *The Second American Revolution*. Elgin, Ill.: David C. Cook, 1982.

Whitehead, John W. *The Separation Illusion*. Milford, Mich.: Mott Media, 1977.

Wrong, George M. *The Conquest of New France*. New Haven: University Press, 1918.

Young, Alexander. *Chronicles of The Pilgrim Fathers of The Colony of Plymouth: 1602-1625*. Boston: Charles C. Little and James Brown, 1841.

Picture Credits

Suggestions for a
Basic Home Library

The following list of books is offered as the basis of study which will greatly expand the individual's knowledge of the Christian principles discussed in this guide. It is, however, only a basic list and is not intended to be complete. The emphasis is on books that are currently available, either in bookstores or public libraries. As the individual grows in knowledge of Scriptures and their application to all areas of life, he will come to know which area of study is best for him; his library will expand accordingly. Other areas of study should not be neglected, however, as a well-rounded education in Biblical principles and their historic development and application is important to all who seek to restore America's eroded Biblical foundations.

Basic Bible Study Aids

Thompson Chain Reference Bible.
Thayer's Greek English Lexicon, in paperback.
An Interlinear Greek-English New Testament, in paperback.
Strong's Exhaustive Concordance, in paperback.
Matthew Henry's Commentary on the Bible, in 6 volumes, or John Gill's
    Commentary on the Bible, in 6 volumes.

American History and Government

Baldwin, Alice M. *The New England Clergy and the American Revolution.*
    New York: Frederick Ungar Publishing Co., 1958. An invaluable book on
    the influence of the New England clergy on the body politic prior to and
    during the Revolution. Look for it in your local library or an old book
    store.
Bartlett, Robert Merrill. *The Pilgrim Way.* Philadelphia: United Church
    Press, 1971. An excellent work on the Pilgrims, particularly their pastor,
    Rev. John Robinson. Written by a Pilgrim descendant. Available from the
    book shop at Plimoth Plantation, Box 1620, Plymouth, Mass. 12360.

Bradford, William. *Of Plymouth Plantation – 1620-1647*. With Notes and Introduction by Samuel Eliot Morison. The Modern Library. New York: Random House, 1967. A good edition frequently to be found on local library shelves.

Brown, John. *The Pilgrim Fathers of New England and Their Puritan Successors*. Pasadena, Texas: Pilgrim Publications, 1970. A moving account of the Pilgrims from their beginnings in England through the early years in New England with some material on the rise of the Puritan colony of Massachusetts Bay.

D'Aubigne, J. H. Merle. *The Reformation in England*. Vol. 1. Carlisle, Pennsylvania: The Banner of Truth Trust, P. O. Box 621, 1977. Classic history first published in 1853. Helpful reading.

DeMar, Gary. *God and Government: A Biblical and Historical Study*. Atlanta, Georgia: The American Vision, 1982. A 10-lesson, self-study workbook that traces what the Bible teaches about types of government. Illustrated. Addresses many of the questions concerned Christians often ask: What is the Biblical and constitutional view of church/state relations? What are the duties and limitations of civil government? Write to The American Vision, P. O. Box 720515, Atlanta, Georgia 30328.

Hall, Verna M., Comp. *The Christian History of the Constitution of the United States of America: Christian Self-Government with Union*. San Francisco: Foundation for American Christian Education, 1976. A valuable companion volume to CHOC containing many documents tracing the colonists' steps toward union.

Hall, Verna M., Comp. *The Christian History of the American Revolution: Consider and Ponder*. San Francisco: Foundation for American Christian Education, 1979. Unique compilation of historical documents on the Revolution including numerous sermons and extended extracts from two histories of the Revolution, Mercy Otis Warren's, representing a New England viewpoint, and David Ramsey's, written from the Southern point of view. Fascinating reading.

Both *Self-Government with Union* and *Consider and Ponder* may be obtained from the Foundation for American Christian Education at P. O. Box 27035, San Francisco, 94127.

Hamilton, Alexander; Jay, John; Madison, James. *The Federalist*. Available in many editions. Must reading for every American who desires to understand America's unique dual system of government.

Jaspers, Glen A. and Smith, Ruth Jaspers. *Restoring America's Heritage of Pastoral Leadership*. Marshalltown, Iowa: 1982. A fine study guide for pastors who want to understand the Biblical principles of the colonial ministers and how they led their congregations into a proper understanding of self- and civil government in accordance with the laws of God. By a minister and an outstanding Christian educator. Write to: The Pilgrim Institute, P. O. Box 932, Marshalltown, Iowa 50158.

Latourette, Kenneth Scott. A History of Christianity. Vol. 2: A.D. 1500-A.D. 1975. Revised edition. New York, Hagerstown, San Francisco, London: Harper & Row, Publishers, 1953. Paperback. Excellent overview of the Reformation tracing the growth of Christianity in Europe and the United States.

Locke, John. Two Treatises of Government. A Critical Edition with Introduction by Peter Laslett. A good paperback edition of this excellent work with many helpful notes is available from The New American Library, P. O. Box 2310, Grand Central Station, New York. N.Y. 10017.

Marshall, Peter, and Manuel, David. The Light and the Glory. Old Tappan, New Jersey: Fleming H. Revell Co., 1977. The story of God's hand throughout our history; a well-researched and very readable account. Available at your local Bible book store.

McDonald, Lawrence P. We Hold These Truths. Seal Beach, Calif.: '76 Press, 1976. Useful paperback; details history of the Constitution and current violations with suggestions for corrective action.

Morgan, Edmund S. The Puritan Family. Harper Torchbooks. New York: Harper and Row. A good paperback edition. A beautiful account of the Puritan philosophy of life by an outstanding scholar. Also may often be found in public libraries.

Robinson, Stewart. "And...We Mutually Pledge..." New Canann, Conn.: The Long House, Inc., 1964. A fascinating account of the influence of the colonial clergy on the drafting of the Declaration of Independence with many extracts of sermons written at the time. Write to the publishers at: Box 3, New Canaan, Conn.

Tocqueville, Alexis de. Democracy in America. 2 vols. Translated by Henry Reeve and revised by Francis Bowen. Edited by Phillips Bradley. New York: Vintage Books, Inc., 1955. A good paperback edition of this remarkably perceptive account of American institutions, government and politics by a foreign observer writing in the 1830's. De Tocqueville's analysis of the virtues of the American system and the pitfalls lying in its path has many important insights for us today.

Walton, Rus. Fundamentals for American Christians. Marlborough, New Hampshire: Plymouth Rock Foundation, 1978. A study manual rich with Biblical documentation and governmental insight. Excellent study aid on the Biblical principles that are the foundation of our nation. Available from the Plymouth Rock Foundation, P. O. Box 425, Marlborough, New Hampshire 03455.

Biographies

John Adams

A Biography in His Own Words. 2 vols. James Bishop Peabody, ed., with an Introduction by L. H. Butterfield, ed. in chief, The Adams Papers. *The Founding Fathers Series.* New York: Newsweek Book Division, 1973. Much useful historical biographical material in a condensed form. Still can be found in some bookstores.

The Book of Abigail and John. Selected Letters of The Adams Family 1762-1784, edited and with an introduction by L. H. Butterfield, Marc Friedlaender and Mary-Jo Kline. Cambridge, Mass. and London, England: Harvard University Press, 1975; 6th printing, 1977. Paperback. Generally available in bookstores. Provides fascinating insights into the mind of this outstanding Founding Father and his remarkable wife. Their letters show their deep faith in Divine Providence, and their serious approach to the education of their children in divine precepts.

William Bradford

Smith, Bradford. *Bradford of Plymouth.* Philadelphia and New York: J. B. Lippincott Co., 1951. Well written in easy, popular style. Frequently may be found in public libraries.

Patrick Henry

Dickson, Norine Campbell. *Patrick Henry: Patriot and Statesman.* New York: The Devin-Adair Co., 1969. Excellent portrayal of an often misunderstood Founding Father. Available from: Fairfax Christian Bookstore, 1121 Pope's Head Road, Fairfax, Virginia 22030.

James Madison

A Biography in His Own Words. 2 vols. Merrill D. Peterson, ed. with an Introduction by Robert A. Rutland. *The Founding Fathers Series.* New York: Newsweek Book Division, 1974. A useful compilation of letters and papers of "the Father of the Constitution."

George Mason

Miller, Helen Hill. *George Mason, Gentleman Revolutionary.* Chapel Hill, N.C.: University of North Carolina Press, 1975. Good study of frequently forgotten Founding Father. Available from book shop at Colonial Williamsburg, Williamsburg, Virginia.

Rutland, Robert. *George Mason: Reluctant Statesman.* Colonial Williamsburg, Inc., Holt, Rinehart and Winston, 1961. Excellent brief biography of the "Father of the Bill of Rights."

George Washington

A Biography in His Own Words. Edited by Ralph K. Andrist with an Introduction by Donald Jackson. *The Founding Fathers Series.* New York: Newsweek Books Division, 1972. Useful compilation of Washington's letter and papers.

Irving, Washington. *George Washington, A Biography.* Edited and abridged by Charles Neider. Garden City, N.Y.: Doubleday and Company, Inc., 1976. Fine condensation of classic biography of Washington by his namesake who was a prominent literary figure in his own right. Very useful. Check bookstores and libraries.

Johnson, William J. *George Washington, The Christian.* Milford, Mich.: Mott Media, 1976. Presents ample historical documentation of the Christian convictions of "the Father of his Country." Available from the publishers at Box 236, Milford, Michigan, 48042. Paperback.

The Maxims of George Washington, Political, Social, Moral, and Religious. Collected and Arranged by John Frederick Schroeder, D.D. Mt. Vernon, Virginia: The Mount Vernon Ladies' Association, 1942. 5th printing, 1974. Excellent breakdown of the thoughts of Washington arranged under subject headings.

Wilbur, William H. *The Making of George Washington.* Caldwell, Idaho, Caxton Printers, 1973. Foreword by Dr. Kenneth D. Wells, President of Freedom's Foundation at Valley Forge. Excellent biography of Washington; highly useful to read to your children. Many details on how Washington was educated and on his own efforts at self-education and character building.

Capitalism and Free Enterprise

Chamberlain, John. *The Roots of Capitalism.* May be obtained from the Foundation for Economic Education, Inc., Irvington-on-Hudson, New York 10533. Shows the importance of the connection between economic thought and practice, and how essential private property is to the effective use of capital.

Chilton, David. *Productive Christians in an Age of Guilt Manipulators. A Biblical Response to Ronald Sider.* Tyler, Texas: Institute for Biblical Economics. A refutation of the claims of certain "evangelical socialists" that the answer to our problems is more government control over every area of life. Write to: The Institute for Christian Economics, P. O. Box 6116, Tyler, Texas 75711.

Gilder, George. *Wealth and Poverty.* New York: Basic Books, Inc., 1981. Provocative economic discussion; very useful. Generally available in book shops.

Hazlitt, Henry. *Economics in One Lesson.* An Arlington House Book. Available from The Foundation for Economic Education, Inc. Irvington-on-Hudson, New York 10533. Completely updated edition of this classic exposition of general economic principles written in laymen's terms. Applies the truths of economics to the problems and opportunities of today and tomorrow.

North, Gary. *Christian Economics.* Nutley, New Jersey: Craig Press, 1976. Excellent basic book on economics from the Christian perspective.

Christian Education

Ballenger, Belinda Beth. *A Family Study on the Life of George Washington.* Columbus, Ohio: Restore America Institute, 1983. A fine Christian scholar details America's traditional method of Biblical reasoning as illustrated in the life of Washington. Write to: Restore America Institute, P. O. Box 23342, Columbus, Ohio 43223.

Jehle, Paul W. *"Go Ye Therefore and Teach."* Marlborough, New Hampshire: Plymouth Rock Foundation. An excellent workbook on how to start a Christian school. Write to: Plymouth Rock Foundation, 6 McKinley Circle (P. O. Box 425) Marlborough, N.H. 03455.

Morris, Barbara M. *Why are you Losing your Children?* Ellicott City, Maryland: The Barbara M. Morris Report, 1976. Useful survey of the promotion of humanism in the public schools. Write to: Barbara M. Morris Report, P. O. Box 412, Ellicott City, Md. 21043.

Rose, James B. *A Guide to American Christian Education for the Home and School — The Principle Approach.* Forthcoming from the American Christian History Institute. Defines and explains the Principle Approach to America's Christian history and government and the philosophy of education used to teach it in the home and school. Write to: American Christian History Institute, 3849 Mural Drive, Claremont, Ca. 91711.

Shafer, Paul W. and Snow, John Howland. *The Turning of the Tides.* New Canaan, Conn.: The Long House, Inc. An expose on the infiltration of socialism into the American public school system. Detailed documentation with list of primary sources. Obtainable from the publisher at Box 3, New Canaan, Conn.

"Symposium on Education," *The Journal of Christian Reconstruction.* Vallecito, California: Chalcedon Foundation. An excellent overview. Write to Chalcedon Foundation, P. O. Box 158, Vallecito, Ca. 95251 for information and a list of other helpful materials.

Church/State Relations

Cord, Robert. *Separation of Church and State: Historical Fact and Current Fiction.* New York: Lambeth Press, 1982. Exhaustive historical documentation of church/state relations in the United States by a distinguished legal scholar.

Whitehead, John W. *The Separation Illusion.* Milford, Michigan: Mott Media, 1977. Explodes the modern notion that our Founders intended a separation of Biblical values from the state.

Whitehead, John W. *The Second American Revolution.* Elgin, Ill.: David C. Cook, 1982. Paperback. Available at your local Bible bookstore. Traces the decline in American society, institutions, and law with particular attention to the First Amendment and its original meaning. A valuable, well-written historical survey.

Cornelison, Isaac A. *The Relation of Religion to Civil Government in the United States of America, a State without a Church But Not without a Religion.* New York and London: G. P. Putnam & Sons, 1895. Very rich vein of documentation on our Biblical roots. Difficult to find except in university libraries.

Morris, B. F. *The Christian Character of the Civil Institutions of the United States.* Philadelphia: G. W. Childs, 1864. Another excellent source for reliable material on church/state relations as conceived by the Founding Fathers. Check libraries.

The Covenant and American Constitutionalism

Elazar, Daniel J. *From Biblical Covenant to Modern Federalism: The Federal Theology Bridge.* Philadelphia: Workshop on Covenant and Politics of the Center for the Study of Federalism, Temple University, 1980.

Elazar, Daniel J. "Political Theory of Covenant: Biblical Origins and Modern Developments." *Publius, The Journal of Federalism.* 10. (Fall 1980). Two penetrating analyses of the importance of the covenant as the basis of American federalism from the Mayflower Compact to the Constitution. Many other useful research papers on covenant principles in American history available from the Center. Write to: Center for the Study of Federalism, Temple University, Philadelphia, Pa. 19122.

McLaughlin, Andrew C. *The Foundations of American Constitutionalism.* New York: Fawcett World Library, 1961. Paperback. Look for in old bookstores. Some libraries will also have in hardcover. An authoritative look at the origins of American Constitutional government with excellent documentation of its covenantal roots.

Miller, Perry. *The New England Mind: The Seventeenth Century.* Boston, Beacon Press, 1968. A good paperback edition of this landmark work which first appeared in 1939. A trailblazer in reawakening interest in the Puritans, their ideals and goals and bringing out the importance of the Puritans' Federal Theology to the building of our body politic.

Newsletters and Reports

Mayflower Institute Journal, published by the Foundation for Christian Self-Government. A semi-monthly devoted to America's Christian history and an update of the movement to restore America to its Biblical moorings. Write to: Mayflower Insitute, P. O. Box 1087, Thousand Oaks, Ca. 91360.

Chalcedon Report, available monthly upon request from the Chalcedon Foundation, P. O. Box 158, Vallecito, Ca. 95251. Deals with contemporary culture in the light of Biblical law.

American Vision Press, P. O. Box 720515, Atlanta, Ga. 30328. A monthly newsletter devoted to the Biblical world view as applied to all areas of life.

The Rock, a quarterly published by the Plymouth Rock Foundation, 6 McKinley Circle, P. O. Box 425, Marlborough, N.H. 03455. Presents the Biblical answers to Communism and socialism. The *Letter from Plymouth Rock* and *FAC Sheet* are published monthly to apply Biblical principles to current issues.

Children's Books

A number of well-written biographies of historical figures like George Washington, Abraham Lincoln, Abigail Adams, Christopher Columbus, Francis Scott Key, Johannes Kepler, George Washington Carver are available from Mott Media, Milford, Michigan 48042. Good for fifth and sixth graders and make excellent material for reading aloud to your children on a family reading night.

Weiner, Rose. *Friends of God.* Gainesville, Fla.: Maranatha Campus Ministries, 1983. Beautiful 9"x12" hardbound, full color book of Bible stories that relate Biblical principles of living in simple terms that even the very young can understand. The stories include question-and-answer paragraphs to increase the child's reading comprehension, concentration and ability to reason. A wonderful teaching tool for parents. To order, write to: Mayflower Institute, P. O. Box 1087, Thousand Oaks, Ca. 91360.

Other Works of General Interest

Brown, Harold O. J. *The Reconstruction of the Republic.* New Rochelle, N.Y.: Arlington House, 1977. In this carefully reasoned book, a leading Christian scholar explodes the fallacy that "religion and politics don't mix," pointing out that Christians took an active part in framing our laws on both the state and federal level. Available from Arlington House Publishers, New Rochelle, New York.

Rushdoony, Rousas J. *The Nature of the American System.* Fairfax, Va.: Thoburn Press, 1978. A Christian philosopher's view of the American system of government. Discusses constitutionalism versus centralism, current attacks on religious liberty, the importance of local self-government.

Rushdoony, Rousas J. *Politics of Guilt and Pity.* Fairfax, Virginia: Thoburn Press, 1978. Contrasts the politics of statism and the politics of responsiblity under God and independence from statism.

Schaeffer, Francis A. *A Christian Manifesto.* Westchester, Illinois: Crossway Books, 1981. Discusses the rights and responsibilities of Christians in America today when confronted with flagrant violations of His laws.

Schaeffer, Francis. A. *Escape from Reason.* Donner's Grove, Illinois: Inter-Varsity Press, 1968. A stimulating history of European art and culture showing the results of a shift from a Christian to a man-centered philosophy.

Schaeffer, Francis, A. *How Should We Then Live? The Rise and Decline of Western Thought and Culture.* Old Tappan, N.J.: Fleming H. Revell Company, 1976. An excellent survey of the impact of the Reformation on Northern Europe and America and the consequences of casting aside our Reformation heritage.

Schaeffer, Franky. *A Time for Anger: The Myth of Neutrality.* Westchester, Illinois: Crossway Books, 1982. Brilliant expose of secular hypocrisy and a moving challenge to Christian faithfulness. The author writes out of his experience as a writer, film maker and artists. Discusses the myth of neutrality in the media, law, politics and the arts. Paperback. Available at your local Bible book store.

Schaeffer, Franky. *Addicted to Mediocrity: 20th Century Christians and the Arts.* Westchester, Illinois: Crossway Books, 1981. Paperback. Available at your local Bible bookstore. In this provocative book, the author shows how Christians have scarificed the artistic prominence they once held and settled instead for bland mediocrity. A demand for excellence in the arts and media and in all areas of life.

Walton, Rus. *One Nation Under God.* Washington, D.C.: Third Century Publishers, 1975. Discusses the Biblical principles underlying American society and institutions and how these principles are being replaced by socialistic and humanistic ideologies. What Christians can do to change the trend. Order from Plymouth Rock Foundation, P. O. Box 425, Marlborough, New Hampshire 03455.